DIFFERENCES

BIBLE

vs.

K^{The}ORAN

The Basic Differences
as Quoted in the Bible and the Koran
That Everyone Should Know

Ben J. Smith

Artisan Publishing
P.O. Box 1529
Muskogee, Oklahoma 74402
(918) 682-8341
www.artisanpublishers.com

All scripture quotations are taken from the Holy Bible: King James Version (except as noted). The Companion Bible published by the American Christian Press, New Knoxville, Ohio, was used as a study tool.

Suras from The Holy Qur-an are taken from the English translation by the Presidency of Islamic Researches, IFTA, CALL and GUIDANCE as presented by King Fahd Ibu Adbul-Azia, King of the Kingdom of Saudi Arabia. This translation has been donated to most public libraries in the United States by the Royal Consulate General of Saudi Arabia.

Published by:

©2002 by Ben J. Smith
All Rights Reserved

Library of Congress card number:
ISBN: 0-934666-64-4

Dedication

This book is dedicated to my wife, Martha, who has been by my side these last 16 years as we have studied the Bible in the original Hebrew and Greek and the various English translations.

The high priority for writing this book was the desire to bring these truths to my family; my children, grandchildren and great-grandchildren.

May this book serve as an enlightenment to them as they face the perilous future and very possibly the last days.

Acknowledgements

First and foremost I want to thank my loving wife Martha. She is the delight of my life and my best friend. It is so great to share the blessings (and infrequent trials) that come our way each day.

It was 15 years ago while living in the Shenandoah Valley of Virginia that we found our pastor through a television dish. We were searching for God's will in our lives and one evening we ran across this minister whose first words we heard were "Even Satan was the son of God." I had never thought of that before, but it sure 'got' my attention. Since that time we have studied with him at least two hours a day. Who is he? Pastor Arnold Murray of the Shepherd's Chapel out of Gravette, Arkansas. He is on Satellite G4-16, twenty-four hours a day, and also on many selected radio stations.

Our major studying tools are: The Companion Bible King James Version, published by the American Christian Press; Green's four volume Interlinear Bible, published by Sovereign Grace and Strong's Exhaustive Concordance and various other translations including the original King James Version of 1611.

I want to thank Lee Heffron (and the patience of her husband, John) for the many hours she devoted to typing, retyping, and coordinating the printing of this book with the publisher.

I extend a special thank you to Hank Hohenstein for proofreading my manuscript and his valuable input towards the completion of the book.

I am also appreciative of the advice and guidance by Mr. Lynn Hoffman of Hoffman Printing for his technical support in producing this book.

*Thy Word is a Lamp Unto My Feet
and a Light Unto My Path*

Psalms 119:105

Contents

Introduction

Since September 11, 2001, many are asking, What is Islam? Is it a peaceful religion? Who was Muhammad? What is the Koran? How does the Koran differ from the Bible? What does the Bible say about these events?

This book was written to give the reader a brief history of the Bible and the Koran. Basically, it is a dictionary of words or subjects, as they are used, and their locations in the Bible or Koran. There is no attempt to interpret or explain the meanings of each verse or sura. Discovery and understanding are up to the reader.

As this book is read, readers should ask themselves the following:

- Is Islam the kind, loving, caring religion it claims to be?
- Is Jesus Christ only a prophet and not the Son of God?
- Is Allah the same god as the God of the Bible?
- Is the Koran a friendly, loving, comforting book?
- Are acts of terrorism around the world justified to promote the cause of Islam?
- Why is American bonded to Israel?
- Is Islam able to peacefully co-exist with the other religions of the world?
- Is Islam a political force hiding behind the religion of Allah?

An in-depth study of the basic differences between the Old and New Testaments and the Koran would fill several volumes. Therefore, this book is only an overview or simple summary of the most salient differences between the two.

This book is written in laymans language with an easy to read style and does not go into multiple interpretations and various doctrinal theories of each. It therefore, becomes a simple outline with quotations from each, leaving the interpretations to the reader. The quotes from the Bible are taken from the King James Version in the Companion Bible and, for the Holy Qur-an, the English translation authorized by "The Presidency of Islamic Research, IFTA, Call of Guidance" and recommended by the Islamic consulate to the United States.

It is also recognized that individual translations of the Bible and Koran do have errors in the translated word or thought that can lead to a misconception of the original intention. An example can be found in the King James Version in Luke 2:1- "there went out a decree from Caesar Augustus that all the world should be taxed." By historical fact Caesar Augustus did not have control of "all the world" and therefore the Greek word, oikoumene, which can be used as world but also can mean land, zone, region or area, should have been translated as land or region. The same mistranslation is found in the story of Noah and the flood in the Old Testament (see Chapter 5, Observations on the Flood).

In the preface of the original Kings James Version of 1611, the 150 scholars assigned to the tremendous task of translating the first English Bible stated that they had done their best to make a factual translation, but there would be discrepancies that each reader should search out for himself.

Since there are many translations of the Koran it must be assumed that certain words, meanings, or thoughts that are used in the translation of this book may vary from the original text.

The Bible and Koran are letters of instruction to the addressed people and therefore, as such, it is most important that the readers know to whom the instructions were written. If one receives a letter by mistake written to some one he does not know, and by someone he does not know, it is of no use to him and surely a waste of time to study its contents. The Bible and Koran were written by different authors, addressed to different people and more importantly, contain a different message.

The Old Testament was specifically written to His Chosen People who were known as the Children of Israel (Jacob) or the Hebrew Children. Reference to "My Chosen People" appears more than 100 times in the Old Testament as God gave His people instructions, corrections, comfort and hope for this life and the life hereafter.

The names of the addressees appear not just a few but many times in the Old Testament and are also referred to many times in the New Testament. It was not written to all, only a select few. The 'Ten Commandments' were given to them along with other health and food laws which they were to follow. God promised to bless them when they obeyed His laws but also would take that blessing away if they did not. When they honored Him, they were blessed; when they turned from Him, they suffered the woes He had promised. Their God did not want them to occupy their neighbors land, only the specific land He had given to Abraham and Isaac and Jacob.

The Old Testament starts with the creation and provides a road map for His people, predicts the coming of the Messiah, promises an eternal resting place and ends with the Judgment of God for the life hereafter.

It tells the story of one man's family, Abraham, and of God's promises to him through his seed of inheritance, Jacob. It relates how Jacob's sons, the Children of Israel, become divided into The House of Judah (the Southern Kingdom) and The House of Israel (the Northern Kingdom), and how each of them were taken into captivity because of their turning to other gods.

God gave Moses the Ten Commandments which forms the basis of western law. Through the Prophets, God warns His people not to worship other gods as the pagans do, and to have no other gods before or after Him. He and He alone was to be their King throughout eternity. God set up a very simple rule. If you follow Me you will prosper. If you turn from Me to other gods, bad things will happen to you because I will withdraw my protection from you. Examples of this simple rule fill the Old Testament to verify that God does bestow His blessing on those who trust in Him and displays His judgment on those who turn to other gods.

The Old Testament was the Bible of Jesus and the Apostles of the New Testament, forming the basic foundation for both the Jewish and Christian faiths.

The New Testament was written only for those who believed that Jesus Christ came as the Messiah as prophesized in the Old Testament. The New Testament was not written to all but to those who have "eyes to see and ears to hear." This phrase appears seven times in the New Testament. Also Jesus Himself said in Matthew 10:6 "But go rather to the lost sheep of the House of Israel (*gentiles*)."

The twenty-seven books of the New Testament were written between 40 and 90 AD by nine godly inspired authors. Luke, the only Greek author, wrote 28 percent and Paul wrote 25 percent of the New Testament. John (who wrote the Gospel of John and Revelations), Peter, and James were three of the twelve disciples of Christ.

The compassionate message of Jesus can best be demonstrated by the Sermon on the Mount, (Matthew 5:2-12) where Jesus said, "Blessed (*happy*) are the poor in spirit (*opposite of proud or haughty*) — Blessed are they that mourn (*for the Lost*) — Blessed are the meek (*humble*) — Blessed are they which do hunger and thirst after righteousness — Blessed are the merciful — Blessed are the pure in heart — Blessed are the peacemakers — Blessed are those who are persecuted for righteousness sake — Blessed are ye, when men shall revile you, and persecute you and shall say all manner of evil against you falsely, for my sake. Rejoice, and be exceedingly glad: for great is your reward in heaven: for so persecuted they the prophets which were before you."

The message of Jesus Christ was not adversarial or vengeful but one of love and peace. In Matthew 5:39-48 Jesus said, to love your enemies, turn the other cheek and go the extra mile. The early Christians (and today's Christians) did not force their beliefs on others by the sword of military might, but by the spiritual sword of the word of God.

The New Testament was written as an extension of the Old Testament with hundreds of references to the Old Testament. Isaiah, alone, was mentioned 85 times in the New Testament. Jesus, Himself said in Matthew 5:17 "Think not that I am come to destroy the law, or the prophets: I am not come to destroy, but to fulfill."

The Koran was written by Muhammad first to the Arabs in Arabia and then expanded to the whole world. It was written on leaves, parchment, leather and wood by Muhammad's followers as he received revelations from an angel he believed to be Gabriel, while in a trance (**Sura 96:1-5**). These revelations came to him over a period of 20 years and were compiled into the Koran some years after his death. The Koran is about the size of the New Testament and the suras (chapters) are placed in the order of their length, the longest being at the beginning, then to the shortest. The 114 suras are not placed in chronological order as Muhammad received them, nor are they placed by subject matter. The Koran is the foundation of Islamic law, religion, culture, and politics.

Muhammad was born in circa 570 AD in the city of Mecca Arabia and died in 632 AD at the age of 62. The first revelation came to him at age 42 and in the next two decades the religion of Islam was formed; most of the tribes of Arabia were converted by military might to Islam and forced to join him and his followers in the conquest and expansion of this new political religion.

The five pillars of Islam are: 1) there is no God but Allah; Muhammad is the Messenger of Allah; 2) prayer performed five times daily facing Mecca, and on Fridays in the mosque; 3) almsgiving, as an offering to Allah and an act of piety; 4) the one month fast of Ramadan; 5) pilgrimage to Mecca.

The Koran teaches the following:
- Muhammad is Allah's prophet above all others (**5:75**)
- Jesus Christ is only a prophet (**5:75**)
  Not the Son of God (**3:59**) (**9:30**) (**10:68-69**) (**19:35**)
  Did not die on the cross (**4:147**)
  Was not resurrected from the dead (**4:158**)
- Mary, Mother of Jesus, sister of Aaron the brother of Moses (**19:27-28**)
- Muhammad came as the Messiah of the Old Testament (**7:158**)
- Muhammad came as the Holy Spirit of the New Testament (**61:6-7**)
- Jews backslid and lost their right to the old covenant (**61:5**)

- Christians backslid and lost their right to the new covenant (**9:30**)
- Believers should not be friends with Jews (Satan) or Christians (infidels) (**5:51**)
- The Koran does not mention The Ten Commandments
- Enemies or adversaries should be killed (**9:73**)
- Other religions should not have right to exist (**2:256**)
- World to be conquered by fighting and military might (**48:27-28**) (**61:9**)
- Men may have four wives (even today) (**4:34**)
- Muhammad can have as many wives as he chooses (**33:51**)
- Unruly wives may be beaten (**4.34**)
- Men should take revenge and not forgive (**3:139-140** and **42:39**)
- Booty of war 20% goes to Muhammad for Allah's good (**8:44**)

From the above list of differences, it is evident that there are fundamental concepts and realities that are dramatically opposite between the God of the Bible and the Allah of the Koran. In the Bible the accounts from God are different from that given by Gabriel to Muhammad. In the Old Testament the lineage of Jacob, the Hebrew Children, are His Chosen People forever, but in the Koran the lineage is through Ishmael and down to Muhammad. The land that God promised Jacob to be his inheritance forever is denied by the revelations to Muhammad. *(NB: This land has now become the major dispute of the Palestinian-Israeli conflict.)*

Continuing, the accounts of the birth and life of Moses are different in each. The God of the Bible in both the Old and New Testaments teaches the "vengeance belongs to God" and that "vengeance is mine." Allah, in the Koran, teaches that the followers must take vengeance 'by the right hand' and kill their oppressors and enemies. Jesus speaking as the Son of God in the New Testament teaches that "we should love our enemies" and "turn the other cheek."

In the New Testament Jesus came to die on the cross and to shed His blood that "whosoever believes on Him should not perish but have everlasting life." In the Koran, Jesus is but a prophet, not the son of God, did not die on the cross, and was not resurrected from the dead. The comforter (Holy Spirit) which Jesus said that He would send would be revealed in the Koran as being Muhammad. The denying of the Holy Spirit by some in the Christian faith is the unpardonable sin.

The accounts leading up to the final judgment are strikingly different. The Judgment Day accounts are different as well as the accounts of Heaven, or Gardens where the virgins await those who have been killed fighting for Allah.

It is therefore evident that the God of the Bible and Allah of the Koran are not the same! God or Gods do not lie. The God of the Bible is not Allah and Allah of the Koran is not the God of the Bible.

Islam started out as a violent religion; to raid, to conquer, to kill and to destroy its neighbors, all in the name of Allah. Within three generations of its founding, it had stretched across three continents defeating the armies of the Persian and Byzantine empires and became the spiritual and political giant of the middle east.

In the last 100 years the giant has been disassembled becoming independent countries Iraq, Iran, Pakistan, Saudi Arabia, etc. Recently the fermentation of the return of Islam to the area and to the world has lead to the terrorism that we are now experiencing in the 21st century. The cycle is repeating — the fear of terrorism and the raids of early Islam is now being used to bring the world to its knees. As the message of Islam is being spread throughout the world to mostly the unlearned or impoverished, it has become todays fastest growing religion with approximately 1.3 billion followers, or one out of every five people on earth are Muslim.

Chapter One

The Bible – Old Testment

The Bible is a library of sacred scriptures of which the Old Testament is the foundation for the New Testament's revelation and Christ's coming. The 39 books of the Old Testament are placed in order of the subject matter: *Pentateuch* (Genesis - Deuteronomy), *Historical Books* (Joshua - Esther), *Poetical Books* (Job, Psalms, Song of Solomon, Lamentations), *Major Prophets* (Isaiah, Jeremiah, Ezekiel, Daniel) and the *Minor Prophets* (Hosea through Malachi).

The Old Testament starts with a story of the beginning of time, dividing the events into days (periods or eons of time) and "creating" mankind on the sixth day. On the seventh day God rested. On the eighth day Adam was "formed" by God, for He found no man to till the field, and still later Eve was formed to provide a helpmate for Adam (**Gen 2**). This was approximately 4000 BC. From their lineage through Seth, came Noah (9 generations to 2950 BC). The Flood (**Chapter 5, Observations**), regional and not world wide, came approximately 2350 BC during the age of pyramid building in Egypt, located less than 800 miles away and confirming that the flood could not have been world wide. The oldest pyramid, the pyramid of Zoser, was built in approximately 2700 BC, some 350 years before the flood. The end of pyramid building came about 2200 BC or 150 years after the flood.

From Noah through his son, Seth, came Abram, later changed to Abraham, eight generations to approximately 2000 BC. At age 50 God spoke to Abram to leave the city of his birth, UR of the Chaldees, and go to the land of Haran. At age 75, God appeared the second time to Abram and instructed him to go into the Land of Canaan. At age 85, Abram's wife, Sarai being barren asked Hagar, her Egyptian maid, to be a surrogate mother for her. When Hagar was with child she despised Sarai, fled the camp and went into the desert, where an angel appeared unto her and told her, "to fear not for of this child — will be a great nation - and he will be a wild man; and his hand will be against every man and every man's hand against him".... (**Gen 16:10-12**). The angel instructed Hagar to return to camp where she gave birth to Ishmael.

It was through the lineage of Ishmael that Islam was founded by Muhammad in the seventh century. A religion that is political and economic in concept, now has one of every five inhabitants of the world as followers.

At age 100 Abram was told by God — And God said unto Abraham "as for Sarai thy wife, thou shalt not call her name Sarai, but Sarah shall her name be. — and I will bless her, and give thee a son also of her: Yea, I will bless her, and she shall be a Mother of Nations: Kings of People shall be of her." — Then Abraham fell upon his face, and laughed, and said in his heart, "Shall a child be born unto him that is an hundred years old? And shall Sarah, that is ninety years old, bear?" — and Abraham said unto God, "O that Ishmael might live before thee!"— and God said, "Sarah thy wife shall bear thee a son indeed; and thou shall call his name Isaac: and I will establish my covenant with him for an everlasting covenant, and with his seed after him — and as for Ishmael, I have heard thee: Behold I have blessed him, and will make him fruitful, and will multiply him exceedingly; twelve princes shall he beget, and I will make him a great nation. — but my covenant will I establish with Isaac, which Sarah shall bear unto thee at this set time in the next year." — and he left off talking with him, and God went up from Abraham (**Gen 17:15-22**).

The Old Testament, was written specifically to the Children of Israel and continues with the story of one man's family and how, through Abraham, two of the great religions of the world were born. With few exceptions all of the writers of the Old Testament were spoken to directly by God, confirmed by more than 500 passages. Moses wrote the first five books (*Pentateuch*) of the Old Testament. There are several books relating to historical facts. The other books were written by the Prophets as they were instructed by God. The Old Testament was written over a span of more than a thousand years from Moses, to the last book of the prophets, Malachi about 433-425 BC.

Abraham was the father of Isaac who married Rebekah and at the age of 40 Rebekah had twin sons, Esau and Jacob. While the twins were still in the womb God said "Jacob I love and Esau I hate" (**Mal 1:3** and **Rom 9:13**). As a young man, Esau caring nothing for his heritage or birthright, sold his birthright to Jacob for a bowl of porridge (*stew*) (**Gen 25:29-34**) and moved east and married the daughter of Ishmael, Mahalath. Later he married Judith and Bashemath both daughters of Hittites (pagans), "which were grief of mind unto Isaac and Rebekah" (**Gen 26:35**).

Jacob was the father of the twelve tribes of Israel. These are Reuben, Simeon, Levi, Judah, Dan, Naphtali, Gad, Asher, Issachar, Zebulun, Joseph and Benjamin. These together are call the Children of Israel or the Hebrew children. And God appeared unto Jacob again and said "Thy name is Jacob: thy name shall not be called anymore Jacob, but Israel shall be thy name." — And God said unto him, "I am God almighty: be fruitful and multiply; a nation and a company of nations shall be of thee, and kings shall come out of thy loins; and the land which I gave Abraham and Isaac, to thee I will give it, and to thy seed after thee will I give the Land." — And Jacob called the name of the place where God spake with him, Beth-el. (**Gen 35:9-15**) (NB: Today's Jerusalem)

From the lineage of Levi came Moses (1571-1451 BC) who led the Children of Israel out of Egypt into the Promised Land. Because of their unbelief and lack of faith, God permitted them to wander in the wilderness for forty years. The generation that came out of Egypt no longer existed, even Moses, when the Children of Israel entered into the land of Canaan. Moses at his death of 120 years gave Joshua the charge of leading the Children of Israel into the Promised Land. Occupying the Promised Land and driving the pagans out, and later to defend it, was the only time in the Bible that God directed his people to go to war from a material and physical standpoint. All other mentions of war, armor, battles, etc. are in the spiritual sense.

Joshua was the first of a series of judges that ruled over Israel from 1452-1000 BC, and God was their king. But the Children of Israel became tired and wanted a king to rule over them as the other countries had. Saul was anointed their king in 1000 BC. He ruled for forty years when David, anointed by God became King. David wrote the Book of Psalms, one of the most beautiful and inspiring books of the Bible. God promised King David that his throne shall be established forever

(II Sam 7:10-16). King David ruled for forty years and at his death his son Solomon was named king.

When Solomon became king he asked God "To know wisdom and knowledge" **(II Chron 1:10-12).** God gave him his desires and thus built the Temple in Jerusalem, wrote the Books of Proverbs and Ecclesiastes and the Song of Solomon and established the most spectacular kingdom of his time. However in spite of his wisdom in later years he turned to the idol worship of his foreign wives, built temples in the high places and turned from God.

Solomon reigned for forty years but upon his death the twelve tribes split into two groups. The "House of Judah" stayed with its capital in Jerusalem, and the "House of Israel" established its capital in Samaria in the North.

The Southern Kingdom was comprised of the tribe of Judah and a portion of the tribe of Benjamin - the "House of Judah." The Northern Kingdom consisted of the other ten tribes and the rest of the tribe of Benjamin - the "House of Israel" or now called "The Ten Lost Tribes." The histories of the two Kingdoms can be found in the books of **I & II Kings, I & II Chronicles.** The two Kingdoms had their own kings and their own agendas and of course fought like the brothers that they were. Both had years when they would turn to God and prosper and then turn away from God and have troubles, only to repeat the cycle. Can it be a lesson for today?

In 610 BC the king of Assyria, Sennacherib, invaded the Northern Kingdom, "The House of Israel" and carried them back as captives to Assyria. They later migrated over the Caucus Mountains and into Western Europe to become the Picts, Gauls, Celts, Anglos, Saxons, etc. and basically the Christian nations of the world. One can easily follow their wanderings by mapping the Dolmids, Menhirs and Stone Circles across Europe. The Scottish declaration of independence states that they have descended from the children of the Hebrews.

Between 496-470 BC Nebuchadnezzar, the King of Babylon invaded the Southern Kingdom and the City of Jerusalem and took the people, the Tribe of Judah, back to Babylon. They were in captivity for seventy years until 426 BC when Cyrus, King of Persia, who had gained control of Babylon, financed their return to Jerusalem to rebuild the temple. At that time they became known as "Jews." (*Carefully note the present day Jew is from the tribe of Judah, "The House of Judah" only, and does not represent the other tribes, "The House of Israel.*")

The Prophets Isaiah, Jeremiah, Ezekiel, and Daniel are known as the greater prophets due to their books being longer than those books of the minor prophets. The minor prophets are Hosea, Joel, Amos, Obadiah, Jonah, Micah, Nahum, Habakkuk, Zephaniah, Haggai, Zechariah, and Malachi. It is important to note that it was God himself who spoke to the writers of the Old Testament, with few exceptions, when an angel appeared. The books of the minor prophets were written from about 690 to 375 BC.

The Old Testament teaches that there will be a Messiah coming to save His people - that there will be a Judgment Day when the Messiah will come to judge the people of the world and then God will set up His Kingdom to reign forever and ever.

Chapter Two

The Bible – New Testament

While the term *testament* can mean "a will," it is more correctly understood in this context in the sense of "a covenant" or "a contract." During His last Passover meal with His disciples, Jesus referred to His death as inaugurating this New Covenant between God and His people (**Luke 22:20**). The appearance of this New Covenant was not unexpected. It had been promised by God through His prophets Jeremiah and Ezekiel about 600 years earlier. Jeremiah promised that this New Covenant would be even more gracious than the Old Covenant that God had made with Moses (**Ex 19:5** & **Deut 7:6**). The New Covenant would place God's law *within* His people, would provide greater intimacy with God and greater knowledge of Him, and would provide final forgiveness of His people's sins (**Jer 31:31-34**). Ezekiel adds that God would also graciously regather Israel, cleanse His people from all their filthiness, and give them a new heart and a new spirit within them, which is His Holy Spirit, who would enable God's people to obey (**Ezek 36:24-27**). (*Quoted from the Liberty Annotated Study Bible - King James Version "Old Time Gospel Hour", Dr. Jerry Falwell, Pastor c1988, Liberty University*)

For God so loved the World, that he gave his only begotten son, that whosoever believeth in him should not perish, but have everlasting life (**John 3:16**). This verse is the essence of the New Testament. God sent Jesus (the Messiah as prophesized in **Isaiah 7:14; 9:6-7**) into this world so that man may have salvation and eternal life. His pre-eminence to all others is found in **I Corinthians 1:14-20**. The New Testament is the road map on how man, as a sinner, may find the assurance that he indeed will have eternal life with God.

The first four books are the gospels of Matthew, Mark, Luke, and John. They each tell of the life of Jesus, but from a different perspective, Matthew — Jehovah as king; Mark — Jehovah as servant; Luke — Jehovah as man; and John - Jehovah as himself. The gospels tell the story of the life of Jesus from His virgin birth by Mary to His death on the cross where He shed His blood for man's sins. The teachings of Christ are told in His own words including the events that are to take place prior to His coming back to set up His eternal kingdom — the New Jerusalem. Many of His teachings were told in parables for those who have "eyes to see and ears to hear."

The Acts of the Apostles, written by the Apostle Luke, records the events of the early church following the death of Christ. The book is divided into two parts, (1) the ministry of Peter, John, Steven, and Phillip (to the people of the land) and (2) the ministry of Paul, Barnabas, and Silas (to the dispersion outside the land). The message is to both the Jews and the Gentiles and records the fulfillment of the Lord's promise to send the Holy Spirit.

The Epistles of Paul were written to both the Jews and Gentiles, explaining the Doctrine of Christ, (by faith in Christ one can be born from above and have eternal life). The Holy Spirit deals with man and that he is justified by faith and not by his works alone. Paul teaches that some are "predestined and them he also called" (**Rom 8** and **9**) but also to the people of free-will "who believe that Jesus is the Son of God shall be saved." (**Rom 10:9**)

The Book of Hebrews was written to the Jews primarily in Jerusalem and to instruct them in Christs' teachings and to break away from their old ways and the sacrifices of the old law. The Messiah of the Old Testament must suffer as man and that Jesus is the Messiah.

The Epistles of Timothy, Titus, Philemon, James, Peter, John, and Jude are books written to individuals, to the Twelve Tribes, to the Diaspora, to his scattered people or to the saints abroad. The theme of the books is to confirm the deity of Christ, to instruct in the teachings of Christ, to give inspiration and encouragement and to warn about the

8

spirit of the anti-Christ. The healing power of Jesus Christ is forcefully brought out in the Book of James.

The Book of Revelations is a message from God spoken directly to John revealing to his 'servants' things which must come to pass in the end times or the Latter Days.

John repeats many times that this was the "Word of God" and confirming that Jesus Christ was the Messiah, the King of Kings and the Lord of Lords. As Jesus spoke during his ministry in parables, so it is as he spoke to John. For example, when speaking of the famine at the end times this is not a famine for food or bread but a famine for the true word of God. In **Amos 8:11** - "I will send a famine in the land, not a famine for bread, nor a thirst for water, but of hearing the words of the Lord." Other examples of metaphors are: Satan, the devil, or the Anti Christ = dragon, serpent, the beast, the little horn; horns = power, rulers or kings; the sword = the word of God; water or seas = people; the dragon = the beast, the serpent; and the little horn = the anti-Christ or the devil.

The book ends with a vivid description of the events that will happen at the end of time. The anti-Christ will be able to make miracles happen on earth and in the skies, bring peace upon the earth for a short time and gain support from the nations of the world. He will gather these nations against Israel and Jerusalem, bringing about the battle of Armageddon and the return of the Lord, Jesus Christ to set up His Kingdom that will last forever and ever.

Chapter Three

The Koran

Muhammad was born in the City of Mecca in Arabia in the year 570 AD. At that time Mecca was the trade center of Arabia and also the religious center for the wandering Bedouins who believed in many deities. The center of worship was the Ka'bah, a cube of a building, legend has it, built by Abraham and his son Ishmael. The Ka'bah housed the images of the various gods and goddesses even including those of Jesus and Mary. It also housed the meteorite black stone which the Muslims now hold in reverence. It is now considered the Holy City of Islam and every Muslim, if finances permit, must visit Mecca at least once in his lifetime.

Muhammad's father died before his birth and his mother died when he was six years old. He was then raised by an uncle who cared for him through his teens. His family was from the wealthy Kuraish tribe who were the custodians of the Ka'bah, enabling Muhammad to spend many hours in the religious circles of the city and he became aware of the vast difference between the idol worship of the Arab Bedouins and the one God of the Christians and Jews. Being a sensitive lad and without father or mother, he spent a great deal of his time alone much of which was in search of God.

At the age of twenty-five Muhammad married Khadijeh, a wealthy widow of 40, who was part of the influential group of the Meccan society. It was not until about age forty that Muhammad received his first vision while meditating alone in a cave. At first he did not realize the impact nor the significance that this would have upon his life. It was not until later that he would become convinced that the visions were the appearances of the angel Gabriel who told him to 'recite'. It is not clear if he could write or if it was his companions who wrote them on the pieces of parchment, bark, leaves, etc. which were eventually gathered to compile what was later to become the Koran.

When Muhammad received his first visions he was reluctant to disclose his feelings to anyone for fear that he may be going mad, but when he told his wife the happenings she encouraged him to continue. She and the family were his first converts. However, converting the City of Mecca and to have the Meccans believe him, would prove to be much different. They would not accept this new religion for fear that it would affect their own system of worship and more importantly, the trade associated with the making of idols and temple worship. The Ka'bah was the central part of their economy and the merchants would not permit anything to disrupt it.

Eventually Muhammad was forced to leave Mecca and move to Yathrib now known as Medina, with about one hundred of his followers who were primarily the outcasts or those not of high rank in the community. This move was later to be called the Hijra in Arabic and started on September 24, 622 AD which is the start of the Muslim calendar. Soon life became financially difficult for him and his followers, but receiving a new vision (**Sura 9:73**) "O prophet strive hard against the unbelievers and the hypocrites, and be firm against them", and as **Sura 9** continues, Muhammad was assured by this revelation that he had been commanded by Allah to strike against the hypocrites or unbelievers.

As he was receiving additional visions, he was becoming more and more convinced that the Jews had lost their covenant with God by their backsliding ways and as "Allah's Prophet" he was the one called to bring chastisement and judgement upon them. He started to raid the caravans of his enemies. These raids, being successful, increased in size and frequency. In the raid at Badr, his band of 350 men massacred over one thousand men, sold their women and children into slavery, with some of the women becoming their wives, and divided the property, once again giving him assurance that truly Allah was with him. He kept twenty percent of the spoils and his men split the rest (**Sura 8:41**); he was becoming richer and more powerful both as a spiritual and political leader.

He was also enlarging his family by taking wives of his men as they fell in battle and his captives' wives and being justified by revelation (**Sura 33:35-52**) of his special privilege of having more than four wives, instead of being limited to four as were the other men (**Sura 4:3**). Muhammad had 10-12 wives (some accounts state more) including the divorced wife of his adopted son, the seven year old daughter of his friend and assistant, Abubakr, and at least three women captured in his raids, whose husbands had been killed.

As his power and riches increased he was able to form a treaty with his former enemies the tribe of Kuraish in Mecca, enabling him and his men to enter freely into the City of Mecca. Two years later, with ten thousand men, he captured the city, executed some of the top leaders, cleansed the temple of the pagan idols and established himself as the religious and political head of the city. He declared "Mecca the City of Allah", center of the Muslim world. Using Mecca as the persuading force he quickly gained the allegiance of the surrounding tribes by giving them the choice of "Allah or death." It was during this time that he received the revelation of **Sura 9:5** "kill those who join other Gods." Muhammad had become not only the religious leader of the country, but the recognized political leader as well. Upon Muhammad's death there was a political struggle resulting in the formation of the two principle Islamic groups, the Shiites and the Sunnites.

Muhammad died in the year 632 AD at the age of 62, only 10 years from the 'Hijra', the move from Mecca in 622 AD. After Muhammad's death his friend and second in command, Abu Bakr, continued the terrorism of the raids which eventually became full scale wars. Under the Caliphs, the religion of Islam became the political force to conquer and defeat the armies of the Sassanian (Persia) and the Byzantine empires and within 50 years had control of an area from Punjab on the east to present day Iraq and Iran. During the following 50 years areas now known as Syria, most of Egypt, across North Africa and most of Spain were controlled by the political, religious forces of Islam.

From the early Islamic terrorism of the raids on single caravans to the conquering of great empires, to the present day, the terror that threatens the world today seems to be replayed, only now, on a much larger and a more sinister scale.

Chapter Four

The Bible | The Koran

Abraham

No mention of Abraham being in Mecca.

Genesis 13:18 Then Abram removed *his* tent, and came and dwelt in the plain of Mamre, which *is* in Hebron, and built there an altar unto the Lord.

Genesis 20:12-14 And yet indeed *she* is my sister; she *is* the daughter of my father, but not the daughter of my mother; and she became my wife. — And it came to pass, when God caused me to wander from my father's house, that I said unto her, This *is* thy kindness which thou shalt shew unto me; at every place whither we shall come, say of me He *is* my brother. — And Abimelech took sheep, and oxen, and menservants, and womenservants, and gave *them* unto Abraham, and restored him Sarah his wife.

Genesis 22:17-18 That in blessing I will bless thee, and in multi-

Abraham

Built Ka'bah in Mecca with Ishmael — the city of peace

Sura 2:124-127 And remember that Abraham was tried by his Lord with certain commands, which he fulfilled: He said: "I will make thee an Imam to the people. He pleaded: "And also (Imams) from my offspring!" He answered: "But my promise is not within the reach evil-doers." — Remember we made the House a place of assembly for men and a place of safety; and take ye the Station of Abraham as a place of prayer; and we covenanted with Abraham and Isma'il. That they should sanctify my House for those who compass it round, or use it as a retreat, or bow, or prostrate themselves (therein in prayer). — And remember Abraham said: "My Lord, make this a City of Peace, and feed its people with fruits, - such of them as believe in Allah and the last day." He said: "(Yea), and such as reject

15

plying I will multiply thy seed as the stars of the heaven, and as the sand which *is* upon the sea shore; and thy seed shall possess the gate of his enemies; — And in thy seed shall all the nations of the earth be blessed; because thou hast obeyed my voice.

faith, - for a while will I grant them their pleasure, but will soon drive them to the torment of fire, - An evil destination (indeed)!" — And remember Abraham and Isma'il raised the foundations of the House (with this prayer): "Our Lord! Accept (this service) from us: for Thou art the all-hearing, the all-knowing."

Sura 14:37 O our Lord! I have made some of my offspring to *dwell in a valley without cultivation,** by Thy Sacred house (Ka'bah): in order, O our Lord, that they may establish regular Prayer: So fill the hearts of some among men with love towards them, and feed them with Fruits: so that they may give thanks. ** This valley is the Meccan valley, where the Muslims believe Abraham build Kaibah with Ishmael.*

Adultery

John 8:2-11 And early in the morning he came again into the temple, and all the people came unto him; and he sat down, and taught them. — And the scribes and Pharisees brought unto him a woman taken in adultery; and when they had set her in the midst, — They say unto him, Master, this woman was taken in adultery, in the very act. — Now Moses in the law commanded us, that such should be stoned: but what sayest thou? — This they said, tempting

Adultery

Sura 4:15 If adultery is proved for married woman through the testimony of four witnesses, then detain them in their house until death takes them or God appoints for them a way.

Sura 24:2 The woman and the man guilty of fornication, - flog each of them with a hundred stripes: let not compassion move you in their case, in a matter prescribed by Allah, if ye believe in Allah and the last day: and let a him, that they might have to accuse him. But Jesus stooped down, and with *his* finger wrote on the ground, *as though he heard them not.* — So when they continued asking him, he lifted up himself, and said unto them, He that is without sin among you, let him first cast a stone at her. — And again he stooped down, and wrote on the ground. — And they which heard *it,* being convicted by *their own* conscience, went out one by one, beginning at the eldest, *even* unto the last: and Jesus was left alone, and the woman standing in the midst. — When Jesus had lifted up himself, and saw none but the woman, he said unto her, Woman, where are those thine accusers? hath no man condemned thee? — She said, No man Lord. And Jesus said unto her, Neither do I condemn thee: go, and sin no more.

Allah

Not mentioned in the Bible.
Apparently Allah is a different God than the God of the Bible. Allah does not have a son-Jesus Christ and did not send the Holy Spirit as a Comforter to His people. For other comparisons see headings under Enemies, God, Heaven, Hell, Jesus, Unbelievers, Vengeance and War.

party of the believers witness their punishment.

Allah - *Can Blot You Out and Bring a New Creation*

Sura 14:19 Seest thou not that Allah created the heavens and the earth in truth? If He so will, He can remove you and put (in your place) a new creation?

Sura 35:16 If He so pleased, He could blot you out and bring in a new creation.

17

Allah - _Forsaking Allah is to accept Satan_

Sura 4:119-121 "I will mislead them, and I will create in them false desires; I will order them to slit the ears of cattle, and to deface the (fair) nature created by Allah," whoever, forsaking Allah, takes Satan for a friend, hath of a surety suffered a loss that is manifest. — Satan makes them promises, and creates in them false hopes, but Satan's promises are nothing but deception. — They (his dupes) will have their dwelling in Hell, and from it they will find no way of escape.

Allah - _Has No Son_

Sura 17:111 Say: "Praise be to Allah, who begets no son, and has no partner in (his) dominion: nor (needs) He any to protect Him from humiliation: yea, magnify Him for His greatness and glory!"

Sura 72:3 'And exalted is the majesty of our Lord: He has taken neither a wife nor a son.

Sura 112:3 He begetteth not, nor is he begotten;

Allah - _Not a Trinity_

Sura 4:171 O People of the Book! Commit no excesses in your religion: nor say of Allah aught but the truth. Christ Jesus the son of Mary was (no more than) a Messenger of

Allah, and His word, which He bestowed on Mary, and a spirit proceeding from Him: so believe in Allah and his Messengers. Say not "Three": desist: it will be better for you: For Allah is one God: glory be to Him: (far exalted is He) above having a son. To Him belong all things in the heavens and on earth. And enough is Allah as a disposer of affairs.

Allah - *Strive and Fight*

Sura 4:95 Not equal are those believers who sit (at home), except those who are disabled. And those who strive and fight in the cause of Allah with their goods and their persons. Allah hath granted a grade higher to those who strive and fight with their goods and persons than to those who sit (at home). Unto all (in faith) hath Allah promised good: but those who strive and fight hath He distinguished above those who sit (at home) by a great reward.

Alliance

NB: The Bible does not specifically teach against ethnic groups.

II Corinthians 6:14 Be ye not unequally yoked together with unbelievers: for what fellowship hath righteousness with unrighteousness? and what communion hath light with darkness?

Alliances - *Christians and Jews*

Sura 5:51 Oh ye who believe! Take not the Jews and the Christians for your friends and protectors: they are but friends and protectors to each other. And he amongst you that turns to them (for friendship) is of them. Verily Allah guideth not a people unjust.

Animal Sacrifice

Old Testament stopped when the Temple was destroyed in 70 AD. New Testament Jesus Christ became the sacrifice for the sins of the world, by shedding His blood on the cross.

I Corinthians 5:7 Purge out therefore the old leaven, that ye may be a new lump, as ye are unleavened. For even Christ our passover is sacrificed for us:

Matthew 26:28 For this is my blood of the new testament, which is shed for many for the remission of sins.

Romans 12:1 I beseech you therefore, brethren, the mercies of God, that ye present your bodies a living sacrifice, holy, acceptable unto God, *which is* your reasonable service.

Armageddon

Zechariah 14:1-4 Behold, the day of the Lord cometh, and thy spoil shall be divided in the midst of thee. — For I will gather all nations against Jerusalem to battle; and the city shall be taken, and the houses rifled, and the women ravished; and half of the city shall go forth into captivity, and the residue of the people shall not be cut off from the city. — Then shall the Lord go forth and fight against those nations as when he fought in the day of battle. — And his feet shall

Animal Sacrifice

Still practiced today especially in the month of Ramadan for the remission of sins.

Armageddon

Not mentioned in the Koran. Possibly referred to as the turmoil prior to the Judgment Day.

stand in that day upon the mount of Olives, which is before Jerusalem on the east, and the mount of Olives shall cleave in the midst thereof toward the east and toward the west, *and there shall be* a great valley; and half of the mountain shall remove toward the north, and half of it toward the south.

Revelation 16:16-21 And he gathered them together into a place called in the Hebrew tongue Armageddon. — And the seventh angel poured out his vial into the air; and there came a great voice out of the temple of heaven, from the throne, saying, It is done. — And there were voices, and thunders, and lightnings; and there was a great earthquake, such as was not since men were upon the earth, so mighty an earthquake, *and* so great. — And the great city was divided into three parts, and the cities of the nations fell: and great Babylon came in remembrance before God, to give unto her the cup of the wine of the fierceness of his wrath. — And every island fled away, and the mountains were not found. — And there fell upon men a great hail out of heaven, *every stone* about the weight of a talent: and men blasphemed God because of the plague of the hail; for the plague thereof was exceeding great.

Armor of God
Ephesians 6:13-17 Wherefore

Armor
Although armor is not mentioned in

take unto you the whole armour of God, that ye may be able to withstand in the evil day, and having done all, to stand. — Stand therefore, having your loins girt about the truth, and having on the breastplate of righteousness: — And your feet shod with the preparation of the gospel of peace; — Above all, taking the shield of faith, wherewith ye shall be able to quench all the fiery darts of the wicked. — And take the helmet of salvation, and the sword of the Spirit, which is the word of God:

the Koran it is eluded to in various suras as going to a physical war against the unbelievers (enemies).
The concept of putting on a 'spiritual armor' is non-existent. (See Unbelievers, War)

Booty

The concept of booty taken from captives appears in the Old Testament as the Children of Israel occupied the land (Canaan) which God had promised to Abraham, Isaac and Jacob and their fights to keep it. Nowhere does it teach to occupy land that was not previously promised by God. In the New Testament the concept of taking booty (material items) in war is offset by taking the sword (the word of God) to the uttermost part of the world.

Booty

Sura 8:1 They ask thee concerning (things taken as) spoils of war. Say: "(Such) spoils are at the disposal of Allah and the Messenger: so fear Allah, and keep straight the relations between yourselves: obey Allah and his Messenger, if ye do believe."

Sura 8:41 And know that out of all the booty that ye may acquire (in war), a fifth share is assigned to Allah, - and to the Messenger, and to near relatives, orphans, the needy, and the wayfarer, - If ye do believe in Allah and in the revelation we sent down to our servant on the day of discrimination - the day of the meeting of the two forces. For Allah hath power over all things.

22

Sura 8:69 But (now) enjoy what ye took in war, lawful and good: but fear Allah: for Allah is oft-forgiving, most merciful.

Sura: 48:15-16 Those who lagged behind (will say), when ye set forth to acquire booty (in war): "permit us to follow you." They wish to change Allah's word; say: "Not thus will ye follow us: Allah has already declared (this) beforehand": then they will say, "But ye are jealous of us." Nay, but little do they understand (such things.) — Say to the desert Arabs who lagged behind: "Ye shall be summoned (to fight) against a people given to vehement war: then shall ye fight, or they shall submit. Then if ye show obedience, Allah will grant you a goodly reward, but if ye turn back as ye did before, He will punish you with a grievous chastisement."

Sura 59:7 What Allah has bestowed on his Messenger (and taken away) from people of the townships, - belongs to Allah, - to his Messenger, and to kindred and orphans, the needy and the wayfarer; in order that it may not (merely) make a circuit between the wealthy among you. So take what the Messenger gives you, and refrain from what he prohibits you. And fear Allah; for Allah is strict in punishment.

Comforter
(The Holy Spirit)

John 14:16 And I will pray the Father, and he shall give you another Comforter, that he may abide with you for ever;

John 14:26 But the Comforter, *which is* the Holy Ghost, whom the Father will send in my name, he shall teach you all things, and bring all things to your remembrance, whatsoever I have said unto you.

John 15:26 But when the Comforter is come, whom I will send unto you from the Father, *even* the Spirit of truth, which proceedeth from the Father, he shall testify of me:

John 16:7 Nevertheless I tell you the truth; It is expedient for you that I go away: for if I go not away, the Comforter will not come unto you; but if I depart, I will send him unto you.

Matthew 12:31-32 Wherefore I say unto you, All manner of sin and blasphemy shall be forgiven unto men: but the blasphemy against the *Holy* Ghost shall not be forgiven unto men. — And whosoever speaketh a word against the Son of man, it shall be forgiven him: but whosoever speaketh against the Holy Ghost, it shall not be forgiven him, neither in this world, neither in the *world* to come.

Comforter - *Holy Spirit*
Muhammad takes the place of Ahmad (Holy Spirit).

Sura 61:6 And remember, Jesus, the son of Mary, said: "O Children of Israel! I am the messenger of Allah (sent) to you, confirming the Taurat (which came) before me, and giving glad tidings of a messenger to come after me, whose name shall be Ahmad." But when he came to them with clear signs, they said, "This is evident sorcery!"

24

Matthew 28:19 Go ye therefore, and teach all nations, baptizing them in the name of the Father, and of the Son, and of the Holy Ghost:

Mark 3:29 But he that shall blaspheme against the Holy Ghost hath never forgiveness, but is in danger of eternal damnation:

Luke 11:13 If ye then, being evil, know how to give good gifts unto your children: how much more shall *your* heavenly Father give the Holy Spirit to them that ask him?

I John 5:7 For there are three that bear record in heaven, the Father, the Word, and the Holy Ghost: and these three are one.

Creation

Genesis 1:27 "So God created man in His *own* image; in the image of God He created him; male and female He created them."

Genesis 2:7 "And the Lord God formed man *of* the dust of the ground, and breathed into his nostrils the breath of life; and man became a living being."

Isaiah 43:7 "Everyone who is called by My name, whom I have created for My glory; I have formed him, yes, I have made him."

Creation

Sura 22:5 O mankind, if ye have a doubt about the resurrection, (consider) that we created you out of dust, then out of sperm, then out of leech-like clot, then out of a morsel of flesh, partly formed and partly unformed, in order that we may manifest (our power) to you; and we cause whom we will to rest in the wombs for an appointed term, then do we bring you out as babes, then (foster you) that ye may reach your age of full strength; and some of you are called to die, and some are sent back to the feeblest old age, so that they know nothing after having known (much). ...

Sura 23:12-14 Man we did create from a quintessence (of clay) — Then we placed him as (a drop of) sperm in a place of rest, firmly fixed; — Then we made the sperm into a clot of congealed blood; then of that clot we made a (foetus) lump; then we made out of that lump bones and clothed the bones with flesh; then we developed out of it another creature. So blessed by Allah, the best to create!

Enemies

Luke 6:27 But I say unto you which hear, Love your enemies, do good to them which hate you,

Luke 6:35 But love ye your enemies, and do good, and lend, hoping for nothing again; and your reward shall be great, and ye shall be the children of the Highest: for he is kind unto the unthankful and *to* the evil.

Matthew 5:38-48 Ye have heard that it hath been said, An eye for an eye, and a tooth for a tooth: — But I say unto you, That ye resist not evil: but whosoever shall smite thee on thy right cheek, turn to him the other also. — And if any man will sue thee at the law, and take away thy coat, let him have *thy* cloak also. — And whosoever shall compel thee to go a mile, go with him twain. — Give to him that asketh thee, and from him that would borrow of thee turn not

Enemies

(See Unbelievers)

Sura 2:191-193 And slay them wherever ye catch them and turn them out from where they have turned you out; for persecution is worse than slaughter; but fight them not at the Sacred Mosque, unless they (first) fight you there; but if they fight you, slay them. Such is the reward of those who reject faith — But if they cease, Allah is oft-forgiving, most merciful. — And fight them on until there is no more persecution and the religion becomes Allah's. But if they cease, let there be no hostility except to those who practice oppression.

Sura 4:101 When ye travel through the earth, there is no blame on you if ye shorten your prayers, for fear the unbelievers may attack you: for the unbelievers are unto you open enemies.

thou away. — Ye have heard that it hath been said, Thou shalt love thy neighbour, and hate thine enemy. — But I say unto you, Love your enemies, bless them what curse you, do good to them that hate you, and pray for them which despitefully use you, and persecute you; — That ye may be the children of your Father which is in heaven: for he maketh his sun to rise on the evil and on the good, and sendeth rain on the just and on the unjust. — For if ye love them which love you, what reward have ye? do not even the publican the same? — And if ye salute your brethren only what do ye more *than others?* do not even the publicans so? — Be ye therefore perfect, even as your Father which is in heaven is perfect.

Romans 12:20-21 Therefore if thine enemy hunger, feed him; if he thirst, give him drink: for in so doing thou shalt heap coals of fire on his head.——Be not overcome of evil, but overcome evil with good.

Faith

Acts 20:20-21 "How I kept back nothing that was helpful, but proclaimed it to you, — Testifying to Jews, and also to Greeks, repentance toward God and faith toward our Lord Jesus Christ."

Ephesians 2:8-9 "For by grace you have been saved through faith,

Sura 8:59-60 Let not unbelievers think that they have escaped, they will never frustrate (them). — Against them make ready your strength to the utmost of your power, including steeds of war, to strike terror into (the hearts of) the enemies, of Allah and your enemies, and others besides, whom ye may not know, but whom Allah doth know. Whatever ye shall spend in the cause of Allah, shall be repaid unto you, and ye shall not be treated unjustly.

Faith

The New Testament teaching that, by the grace of God through Faith in Him, one can be saved and obtain eternal life, does not appear in the Koran. Rather it is ones willingness to fight and die for Allah, and his good works that assures his place in the Garden (see Heaven).

27

and that not of yourselves; *it is* the gift of God, — Not of works, lest anyone should boast."

II Timothy 3:15-16 "And that from childhood you have known the Holy Scriptures, which are able to make you wise for salvation through faith which is Christ Jesus. — All Scripture *is* given by inspiration of God, and is profitable for doctrine, for reproof, for correction, for instruction in righteousness,"

Hebrews 11:6 "But without faith *it* is impossible to please *Him* for he who comes to God must believe that He is, and *that* He is a rewarder of those who diligently seek Him."

Garden of Eden
*(Different accounts; For a complete account see **Genesis Chapters 2 and 3**) God blessed the seventh day (**Gen 2:2**). The eighth day God had no man to till the ground (**Gen 2:5**). He then formed man (not created) and the man became a living soul (**Gen 2:7**). He put the man whom He had formed in the Garden of Eden (**Gen 2:8**). In the garden He put the tree of life and the tree of good and evil (**Gen 2:9**). — But do not eat of the tree of good and evil or thou shall surely die (**Gen 2:17**). God formed Eve for a helpmate for Adam (**Gen 2:21-24**). In Chapter Three the serpent beguiled Eve (**Gen***

Garden of Eden
(Different accounts)
Sura 2:30-39 Behold, thy Lord said to the angels; "I will create a vicegerent on earth." They said: "Wilt Thou place therein one who will make mischief therein and shed blood? - whilst we do celebrate Thy praises and glorify Thy holy (name)?" He said: "I know what ye know not" — And He taught Adam the names of all things; then He placed them before the angels, and said: "Tell Me the names of these if ye are right." — They said: "Glory to Thee: of knowledge we have none, save what Thou hast taught us: in truth

3:13) *to partake of the tree of good and evil and Adam followed. They then sewed fig leaves together to cover their nakedness* (**Gen 3:7**). *They knew that they had sinned. God's chastisement for Eve was labor at child birth; for Adam to work the ground by the sweat of thy face and God drove Adam and Eve out of the Garden of Eden* (**Gen 3: 23-34**).

it is Thou who art perfect in knowledge and wisdom." — He said: "O Adam! tell them their names." When he had told them their names, Allah said: "Did I not tell you that I know the secrets of heaven and earth, and I know what ye reveal. And what ye conceal?" — And behold, we said to the angels: "Bow down to Adam:" and they bowed down: not so Iblis: (Satan) he refused and was haughty: he was of those who reject faith. — And we said: "O Adam! dwell thou and thy wife in the garden; and eat of the bountiful things therein as (where and when) ye will; but approach not this tree, or ye run into harm and transgression." — Then did Satan make them slip from the (garden), and get them out of the state (of felicity) in which they had been. And we said: "Get ye down, all (ye people), with enmity between yourselves. On earth will be your dwelling place and your means of livelihood for a time." — Then learnt Adam from his Lord certain words and his Lord turned towards him; for He is oft-returning, most merciful. — We said: "Get ye down all from here; and if, as is sure, there comes to you guidance from Me, whosoever follows my guidance, on them shall be no fear, nor shall they grieve. — "But those who reject faith and belie our signs, they shall be companions of the fire; they shall abide therein."

God - Himself

Deuteronomy 32:4 *He is* the Rock, his work *is* perfect: for all his ways *are* judgment: a God of truth and without iniquity, just and right *is* he.

Isaiah 45:21-25 "...And *there is* no other God besides Me, a just God and a Savior; *there* is none besides Me. - Look to Me, and be saved, all you ends of the earth: For I *am* God, and *there* is none else." - I have sworn by myself, the word is gone out of my mouth *in* righteousness, and shall not return, That unto me every knee shall bow, every tongue shall swear. - Surely, shall *one* say, in the Lord have I righteousness and strength: *even* to him shall *men* come; and all that are incensed against him shall be ashamed. - In the Lord shall all the seed of Israel be justified, and shall glory.

Psalms 99:9 "...for the Lord our God is holy."

I Timothy 1:17 "Now to the King eternal, immortal, invisible, to God who alone is wise, *be* honor and glory forever and ever. Amen."

God's Children

I John 3:2 Beloved, now are we the sons of God, and it doth not yet appear what we shall be: but we know that, when he shall appear, we shall be like him; for we shall see him as he is.

God Himself

There is no god but Allah, Most Gracious Most Merciful, appears in most Suras of the Koran.

God's Children

Sura 5:18 (Both) the Jews and the Christians say: "We are sons of Allah, and His beloved," Say: "Why then doth He punish you for your sins? Nay, ye are but men - of the men. He hath created: He for-

30

God's Love

John 3:16 For God so loved the world that He gave His only begotten Son, that whosoever believeth in him should not perish, but have everlasting life.

Romans 5:8 But God commendeth his love toward us, in that, while we were yet sinners, Christ died for us.

God's Love For His Son Jesus

John 5:19-23 Then answered Jesus and said unto them, Verily, verily, I say unto you, The Son can do nothing of himself, but what he seeth the Father do: for what things soever he doeth, these also doeth the Son likewise. — For the Father loveth the Son, and sheweth him all things that himself doeth: and he will shew him greater works than these, that ye may marvel. — For as the Father raiseth up the dead, and quickeneth *them*; even so the Son quickeneth whom he will.

God's Nature

John 3:16 For God so loved the world that He gave His only begotten Son, that whosoever believeth in him should not perish, but have everlasting life.

John 5:24 Verily, verily, I say unto you, He that heareth my word, and believeth on him that sent me, hath everlasting life, and shall not come

giveth whom He pleaseth, and he punisheth whom He pleaseth: and to Allah belongeth the dominion of the heavens and the earth, and all that is between: and unto Him is the final goal (of all)"

God's Love

The concept that Allah does not love sinners is repeated twenty-four times in the Koran.

Sura 2:190 Fight in the cause of Allah those who fight you, but do not transgress limits; for Allah loveth not transgressors.

God's Nature

Sura 3:32, 57 Obey Allah and his messenger: But if they turn back, *Allah loveth not those who reject Faith*...As to those who believe and work righteousness, Allah will pay them (in full) their reward: But *Allah loveth not those who do wrong.*

into condemnation; but is passed from death unto life.

John 6:38-40 For I came down from heaven, not to do mine own will, but the will of him that sent me. — And this is the Father's will which hath sent me, that of all which he hath given me I should lose nothing, but should raise it up again at the last day. — And this is the will of him that sent me, that every one which seeth the Son, and believeth on him, may have everlasting life: and I will raise him up at the last day.

Healing
Mentioned many times in both the Old and New Testaments.

Genesis 20:17 So Abraham prayed unto God: and God healed Abimelech and his wife, and his maidservants; and they bare *children.*

Psalms 30:2 O Lord my God, I cried unto thee, and thou hast healed me.

Jeremiah 30:17 For I will restore health unto thee, and I will heal thee of thy wounds, saith the Lord; because they called thee an Outcast, *saying,* This is Zion, whom no man seeketh after.

Matthew 10:1 And when he had called unto *him* his twelve disciples,

Healing
No mention of healing for followers or of Allah's power to heal.

he gave them power *against* unclean spirits, to cast them out, and to heal all manner of sickness and all manner of disease.

Mark 3:14-15 And he ordained twelve, that they should be with him, and that he might send them forth to preach, — And to have power to heal sicknesses, and to cast out devils:

Luke 5:15 But so much the more went there a fame abroad of him: and great multitudes came together to hear, and to be healed by him of their infirmities.

Luke 6:17-19 And he came down with them, and stood in the plain, and the company of his disciples, and a great multitude of people out of all Judaea and Jerusalem, and from the sea coast of Tyre and Sidon, which came to hear him, and to be healed of their diseases; — And they that were vexed with unclean spirits: and they were healed. — And the whole multitude sought to touch him: for there went virtue out of him, and healed *them* all.

Luke 9:2 And he sent them to preach the kingdom of god, and to heal the sick.

Acts 14:8-10 And there sat a certain man at Lystra, impotent in his feet, being a cripple from his mother's womb, who never had walked: — The same heard Paul speak: who stedfastly beholding him, and perceiving that he had faith to be healed, — Said with a loud voice, Stand upright on thy feet. And he leaped and walked.

Acts 28:8 And it came to pass, that the father of Publius lay sick of a fever and of a bloody flux: to whom Paul entered in, and prayed, and laid his hands on him, and healed him.

Heaven
Mark 12:25 For when they rise from the dead, they neither marry, nor are given in marriage; but are as the angels which are in heaven.

John 14: 1-4 Let not your heart be troubled: ye believe in God, believe also in me. — In my Father's house are many mansions: if it were not so, I would have told you. I go to prepare a place for you. — And if I go and prepare a place for you, I will come again, and receive you unto myself; that where I am, there ye may be also.

Revelation 21: 3-4 "And I heard a loud voice from heaven saying, 'Behold, the tabernacle of God *is* with men, and He will dwell with them, and they shall be His people. God Himself will be with them *and be* their god. — And god will wipe away every tear from their

Heaven - *Gardens*
Sura 2:25 But give glad tidings to those who believe and work right-eousness, that their portions is Gardens, beneath which river flow. Every time they are fed with fruits therefrom, they say, "Why, this is what we were fed with before," for they are given things in similitude; and they have therein companions pure (and holy); and they abide therein (forever).

Sura 37:40-49 But the chosen ser-vants of Allah, — For them is a sus-tenance determined. — Fruits; and they (shall enjoy) honour and dig-nity, — In gardens of delight. — Facing each other on raised couches. — Round will be passed to them a cup from a clear-flowing fountain, — Crystal-white of a taste delicious to those who drink (thereof), — Free from headiness; nor will they suffer intoxication eyes; and there shall be no more death, nor sorrow, nor crying. There shall be no more pain, for the former things have passed away."

Revelation 21:27 "But there shall by no means enter it anything that defiles, or causes an abomination or a lie, but only those who are written in the Lamb's Book of Life."

Revelation 22:1-4 And he shewed me a pure river of water of life, clear as crystal, proceeding out of the throne of God and of the Lamb. — In the midst of the street of it, and on either side of the river, *was there* the tree of life, which bare twelve *manner* of fruits, and yielded her fruit every month: and the leaves of the tree *were* for the healing of nations. — And there shall be no more curse: but the throne of God and of the Lamb shall be in it; and his servants shall serve him: — And they shall see his face; and his name *shall* be in their foreheads.

therefrom. — And besides them will be chaste women; restraining their glances, with big eyes (of wonder and beauty). — As if they were (delicate) eggs closely guarded.

Sura 44:51-56 As to the righteous (they will be) in a position of security, — Among gardens and springs; — Dressed in fine silk and in rich brocade, they will face each other; — So; and we shall wed them to maidens with beautiful, big and lustrous eyes. — There can they call for every kind of fruit in peace and security; — Nor will they there taste death, except the first death; and He will preserve them from the chastisement of the blazing fire.

Sura 55:46, 48, 50, 52, 54, 56, 58, 60, 62, 64, 66, 68, 70, 72, 74, 76, 78
But for such fear the time when they will stand before (the judgement seat of) their Lord. There will be two gardens — Abounding in branches; — In them (each) will be two springs flowing (free); — In them will be fruits of every kind, two and two. — They will recline on carpets, whose inner linings will be of rich brocade: the fruit of the gardens will be near (and easy of reach). — In them will be (maidens), chaste, restraining their glances, whom no man or Jinn before them has touched: — Like

unto rubies and coral. — Is there any reward for good other than good? — And besides these two, there are two other gardens, — Dark-green in colour (from plentiful watering). — In them (each) will be two springs pouring forth water in continuous abundance: — In them will be fruits, and dates and pomegranates: — In them will be fair (maidens), good, beautiful; — Maidens restrained (as to their glances), in (goodly) pavilions: — Whom no man or Jinn before them has touched; — Reclining on green cushions and rich carpets of beauty. — Blessed be the name of they Lord, full of majesty, bounty and honour.

Sura 47:15 (Here is) a Parable of the Garden which the righteous are promised: In it are rivers of water incorruptible; *rivers of milk of which the taste never changes; rivers of wine, a joy to those who drink; and rivers of honey pure and clear.* In it there are for them all kinds of fruits; and Grace from their Lord. (Can those in such bliss) be compared to such as shall dwell forever in the Fire, and be given, to drink, boiling water, so that it cuts up their bowels (to pieces)?

Sura 56:15-38 (They will be) on couches encrusted (with gold) and precious stones), — Reclining on them, facing each other. — Round about them will (serve) youths of perpetual (fresh-ness), — With goblets, (shining) beakers, and cups (filled) out of clear-flowing fountains: — No after-ache will they receive there-from nor will they suffer intoxica-tion: — And with fruits, any that they may select; — And the flesh of fowls, and that they may desire. — And (there will be) compan-ions with beautiful, big, and lus-trous eyes — Like unto pearls well-guarded. — A reward for the deeds of their past (life). — No frivolity will they hear therein, nor any mischief, — Only the saying, "Peace! Peace". — The companions of the right hand, what will be the companions of the right hand! — (They will be) among Lote-trees-trees without thorns, — Among Talh trees with flowers (or fruits) piled one above another, — In shade long-extend-ed, — By water flowing constant-ly, — And fruit in abundance. — Whose season is not limited, nor (supply) forbidden, — And on couches raised high. — We have created them of special creation. — And made them virgin-pure (and undefiled), — Full of love (for their mates), equal in age, — For the companions of the right hand. (*See sura 19:61-63; 35:33-35; 36:55-58; 38:49-52; 39:73-75; 43:68-73; 50:31-35; 52:17-24; 83:22-28; 88:8-16; 89:27-30; 92:17-20*).

Hell

(*NB: The Bible gives no vivid description, as does the Koran, of Hell. It simply states many times that the sinners and ungodly will perish in Hell.*)

The Greek word 'apollumi' as translated is to destroy fully, die, lose, mar or perish. It does not mean to live eternally in torment. The concept of living an everlasting life in torment is not found in the original manuscripts of the Bible. Also the translated word perdition, "apoleiai in Greek, is to ruin, loss, damnable, destruction, die, perish, pernicious ways, or waste. Again there is no concept of a continuation of life in hell after death.

John 3:16 For God so loved the world, that he gave his only begotten Son, that whosoever believeth in him should not perish, but have everlasting life.

II Peter 3:7 But the heavens and the earth, which are now, by the same word are kept in store, reserved unto fire against the day of judgment and perdition of ungodly men.

II Peter 3:9 The Lord is not slack concerning his promise, as some men count slackness; but is long-suffering to us-ward, not willing that any should perish, but that all should come to repentance.

Hell

Sura 4:56 Those you reject our signs. We shall soon cast into the fire: as often as their skins are roasted though. We shall change them for fresh skins, that they may taste the chastisement: for Allah is exalted in power, wise.

Sura 11:119 Except those on whom thy Lord hath bestowed His mercy: and for this did He create them: and the word of thy Lord shall be fulfilled: "I will fill Hell with Jinns and men all together."

Sura 14:16-17 In front of such a one is Hell, and he is given, for drink, boiling fetid water. — In gulps will he sip it, but never will he be near swallowing it down his throat; death will come to him from every quarter, yet will he not die; and in front of him will be a chastisement unrelenting.

Sura 14:49-50 And thou wilt see the sinners that day bound together in fetters: — Their garments of liquid pitch, and their faces covered with fire;

Sura 15:44 To it are seven gates: for each of those gates is a (special) class (of sinners) assigned.

Sura 22:19-22 These two antagonists dispute with each other about their Lord: but those who deny (their Lord), for them will be cut

II Thessalonians 1:8-9 "In flaming fire taking vengeance on those who do not know God, and on those who do not obey the gospel of our Lord Jesus Christ. — These shall be punished with everlasting destruction from the presence of the Lord and from the glory of His power." (*Also see the parable of the rich man and Lazarus in Luke 16:19-31.*)

Revelation 20:15 "And anyone not found written in the Book of Life was cast into the lake of fire."

out a garment of fire: over their heads will be poured out boiling water. — With it will be melted what is within their bodies, as well as (their) skins. — In addition there will be maces of iron (to punish) them. — Every time they wish to get away therefrom, from anguish, they will be forced back therein, and (it will be said). "Taste ye the chastisement of burning!"

Sura 25:11-14 Nay, they deny the hour (of the judgment to come): but we have prepared a blazing fire for such as deny the hour: — When it sees them from a place far off, they will hear its fury and its raging sigh. — And when they are cast, bound together, into a constricted place therein, they will plead for destruction there and then! — "This day plead not for a single destruction: plead for destruction oft-repeated!"

Sura 32:20 As to those who are rebellious and wicked, their abode will be the fire: every time they wish to get away therefrom, they will be forced thereinto, and it will be said to them: "Taste ye the chastisement of the fire, the which ye were wont to reject as false."

Sura 37: 53-74 'When we die and become dust and bones, shall we indeed receive rewards and punishments?' — He said: "Would ye like to look down?" — He looked down and saw him in the midst of the fire. — He said: "By Allah! Thou wast little short of bringing me to perdition! —" Had it not been for the grace of my Lord, I should certainly have been among those brought (there)! — "Is it (the case) that we shall not die," — "Except our first death, and that we shall not be punished?" — Verily this is the supreme triumph. — For the like of this let all strive, who wish to strive. — Is that the better entertainment or the Tree of Zaqqum? (Hell) — For we have truly made it (as) a trial for the wrong-doers. — For it is a tree that springs out of the bottom of Hell-fire: — The shoots of its fruit-stalks are like the heads of devils: — Truly they will eat thereof and fill their bellies therewith. — Then on top of that they will be given a mixture made of boiling water. — Then shall their return be to the (blazing) fire. — Truly they found their fathers on the wrong path; — So they (too) were rushed down on their footsteps! — And truly before them, many of the ancients went astray; — But we sent aforetime, among them warners. — Then see what was the end of those who were warned — Except the chosen servants of Allah.

Sura 55:35-44 On you will be sent (O ye evil ones twain!) A flame of fire (to burn) and a (flash of) molten brass no defense will ye have: — Then which of the favours of your Lord will ye deny? — When the sky is rent asunder, and it becomes red like ointment: — Then which of the favours of your Lord will ye deny? — On that day no question will be asked of man or Jinn as to his sin, — Then which of the favours of your Lord will ye deny? — (For) the sinners will be known by their marks: and they will be seized by their forelocks and their feet. — Then which of the favours of your Lord will ye deny? — This is the hell which the sinners deny: — In the midst and in the midst of boiling water will they wander round! — Then which of the favours of your Lord will ye deny? (*See sura 22:19-22; 25:25; 37:62-67; 38:55-58; 44:43-48; 50:30; 56:52-55; 69:25-29; 69:30-37; 74:30-31; 78:21-25; 79:35-39; 89:23-26*)

Ishmael - *Story of Hagar and Ishmael*

Genesis 16:1-16 Now Sarai Abram's wife bare him no children: and she had an handmaid, an Egyptian, whose name was Hagar. — And Sarai said unto Abram, Behold now, the Lord hath restrained me from bearing: I pray thee, go in unto my maid; it may be that I may obtain children by her. And Abram hearkened to the voice of Sarai. — And Sarai Abram's wife took Hagar her maid the Egyptian, after Abram had

Ishmael - *Prophet of God*

Sura 19:54-55 Also mention in the book (the story of) Isma'il: He was (strictly) true to what he promised, and he was a messenger (and) a prophet. — He used to enjoin on his people prayer and zakat (alms) and he was most acceptable in the sight of his Lord. Legend has it that the Kabah in Mecca was built by Abraham and Ishmael. Ishmael's mother Hagar, is not mentioned in the Koran.

dwelt ten years in the land of Canaan, and gave her to her husband Abram to be his wife. — And he went in unto Hagar, and she conceived; and when she saw that she had conceived, her mistress was despised in her eyes. — And Sarai said unto Abram, My wrong be upon thee: I have given my maid into thy bosom; and when she saw that she had conceived, I was despised in her eyes: the Lord judge between me and thee. — But Abram said unto Sarai, Behold, thy maid *is* in thy hand; do to her as it pleaseth thee. And when Sarai dealt hardly with her, she fled from her face. — And the angel of the Lord found her by a fountain of water in the wilderness, by the fountain in the way to Shur. — And he said, Hagar, Sarai's maid, whence camest thou? and wither wilt thou go? And she said, I flee from the face of my mistress, Sarai. — And the angel of the Lord said unto her, Return to thy mistress, and submit thyself under her hands. — And the angel of the Lord said unto her, I will multiply thy seed exceedingly, that it shall not be numbered for multitude. — And the angel of the Lord said unto her, Behold, thou *art* with child, and shalt bear a son, and shalt call his name Ishmael; because the Lord hath heard thy affliction. — And he will be a wild man; his hand *will* be against every man, and every man's hand against him; and he shall dwell in the presence of all his brethren. — And she called the name of the Lord that spake unto her, Thou God seest me: for she said, Have I also here looked after him that seeth me? — Wherefore the well was called Beer-la-hai-roi; behold, it is between Kadesh and Bered. — And Hagar bare Abram a son: and Abram called his son's name, which Hagar bare, Ishmael. — And Abram was fourscore and six years old, when Hagar bare, Ishmael to Abram.

Genesis 21:8-21 And the child grew, and was weaned: and Abraham made a great feast the *same* day that Isaac was weaned. — And Sarah saw the son of Hagar the Egyptian, which she had born unto Abraham, mocking. — Wherefore she said unto Abraham, Cast out this bondwoman and her son: for the son of this bond-woman shall not be heir with my son, *even* with Isaac. — And the thing was very grievous in Abraham's sight because of his son. — And God said unto Abraham, Let it not be grievous in thy sight because of the lad, and because of thy bondwoman; in all that Sarah hath said unto thee, hearken unto her voice; for in Isaac shall thy seed be called. — And also of the son of the bondwoman will I make a nation, because he is thy seed. — And Abraham rose up early in the morning, and took bread, and a bottle of water, and gave *it* to Hagar, putting *it* on her shoulder, and the child, and sent her away: and she departed, and wandered in the wilderness of Beer-sheba. — And the water was spent in the bottle, and she cast the child under one of the shrubs. — And she went, and sat her down over against *him* a good way off, as it were a bowshot: for she said, Let me not see the death of the child. And she sat over against *him,* and lift up her voice, and wept. — And God heard the voice of the lad; and the angel of God called to Hagar out of heaven, and said unto her, What aileth thee, Hagar? fear not; for God hath heard the voice of the lad where he *is.* — Arise, lift up the lad, and hold him in thine hand; for I will make him a great nation. — And God opened her eyes, and she saw a well of water; and she went, and filled the bottle with water, and gave the lad drink. — And God was with the lad; and he grew, and dwelt in the wilderness, and became an archer. — And he dwelt in the wilderness of Paran: and his mother took him a wife out of the land of Egypt.

Islam

The Bible - New Testament was written 500 years before the Koran and therefore is not mentioned.

Islam - *Above All Other Religions*

Sura 2:193 And fight them on until there is no more persecution and the religion becomes Allah's. But if they cease, let there be no hostility except to those who practise oppression.

Sura 9:33 It is He who hath sent His Messenger with guidance and the religion of truth, to cause it to prevail over all religion, even though the pagans may detest (it).

Islam - *The Only Religion*
Sura 3:85 If anyone desires a religion other than Islam (submission to Allah) never will it be accepted of him; and in the hereafter he will be in the ranks of those who have lost.

Sura 8:39 And fight them on until there is no more persecution, and religion becomes Allah's in its entirety but if they cease, verily Allah doth see all that they do.

Sura 48:27-28 Truly did Allah fulfil the vision for His Messenger: Ye shall enter the Sacred Mosque, if Allah wills, with minds secure, heads shaved, hair cut short, and without fear. For He knew what ye knew not, and He granted, besides this, a speedy victory. — It is He who has sent His Messenger with guidance and the religion of truth, to make it prevail over all religion: and enough is Allah for a witness.

Sura 61:9 It is He who has sent His Messenger with guidance and the religion of truth. That He make it prevail over all religion, even though the pagans may detest (it).

Jacob

Jacob, the son of Isaac, the son of Abraham, had twelve sons from whom came the 12 tribes of Israel or the Hebrew Children - or His Chosen People.

Deuteronomy 32:9-10 For the Lord's portion is his people; Jacob *is* the lot of his inheritance. — He found him in a desert land, and in the waste howling wilderness; he led him about, he instructed him, he kept him as the apple of his eye.

Isaiah 41:8-11 But thou, Israel, *art* my servant, Jacob whom I have chosen, the seed of Abraham my friend. — *Thou* whom I have taken from the ends of the earth, and called thee from the chief men thereof, and said unto thee, Thou *art* my servant; I have chosen thee, and not cast thee away. — Fear thou not; for I *am* with thee: be not dismayed; for I *am* thy God: I will strengthen thee; yea, I will help thee; yea, I will uphold thee with the right hand of my righteousness.

Jerusalem

(NB: Jerusalem is an important city at the present due to the Israeli - Palestinian conflict.)

Jerusalem appeared 812 times in the Bible, some excerpts are as follows:

Jacob - *Only a Prophet*

No mention of land promised to Jacob and his seed.

Sura 6:84-85 We gave him Isaac and Jacob: all (three) we guided: and before him, we guided Noah, and among his progeny, David, Solomon, Job, Joseph, Moses, and Aaron: thus do we reward those who do good:

Sura 19:49 When he had turned away from them and from those whom they worshipped besides Allah, we bestowed on him Isaac and Jacob, and each one of them we made a prophet.

Jerusalem

Not mentioned in the Koran - Islam's holy city is Mecca - Jerusalem is important to Islam due to the Israeli-Palestinian conflict.

II Chronicles 6:6 "But I have chosen Jerusalem, that my name might be there; and have chosen David to be over my people Israel."

Ezra 1:3-4 "...and built the house of the Lord God of Israel (he is the God) which *is* in Jerusalem. — for the house of God that *is* in Jerusalem."

Galatians 4:26 "But Jerusalem which is above is free, which is the mother of us all."

Isaiah 62: 1 & 6 "...for Jerusalem's sake I will not rest, until the righteousness thereof go forth as brightness, and the salvation thereof as a lamp that burneth. — I have set watchmen upon thy walls, O Jerusalem, *which* shall never hold their peace day or night: —"

Joel 3:20-21 "But Judah shall dwell forever, and Jerusalem from generation to generation. — For I will cleanse their blood *that* I have not cleansed: for the Lord dwelleth in Zion (Jerusalem)."

I Kings 11:13 "Howbeit I will not rend away all the kingdom; *but* will give one tribe (*Judah*) to thy son for David my servant's sake, and for Jerusalem's sake which I have chosen."

I Kings 11:32 "But he shall have one tribe (*Judah*) for my servant

David's sake, and for Jerusalem's sake, the city which I have chosen out of all the tribes of Israel:"

I Kings 14:21 "...the city which the Lord did choose out of all the tribes of Israel, to put his name there."

Malachi 3:4 "Then shall the offering of Judah and Jerusalem be pleasant unto the Lord, as in the days of old, and as in former years."

Psalms 122:6 "Pray for the peace of Jerusalem: they shall prosper that love thee."

Zechariah 1:17 "...and the Lord shall yet comfort Zion, and shall yet choose Jerusalem."

Zechariah 12:2, 3, 8, 9 "Behold, I will make Jerusalem a cup of trembling unto all the people round about, when they shall be in the siege both against Judah *and* against Jerusalem. — And in that day will I make Jerusalem a burdensome stone for all people: all that burden themselves with it shall be cut in pieces, though all the people of the earth be gathered together against it. — In that day shall the Lord defend the inhabitants of Jerusalem; — ...in that day, *that* I will seek to destroy all the nations that come against Jerusalem." (*See* **Zechariah Chapters 12** through **14**)

Romans 15:31 "That I may be delivered from them that do not believe in Judaea; and that my service which I *have* for Jerusalem may be accepted of the saints;"

Jesus Christ - His Advent

Isaiah 9:6-7 For unto us a child is born, unto us a son is given: and the government shall be upon his shoulder: and his name shall be called Wonderful, Counsellor, The mighty God, The everlasting Father, The Prince of Peace. — Of the increase of his government and peace *there shall be* no end, upon the throne of David, and upon his kingdom, to order it, and to establish it with judgment and with justice from henceforth even for ever. The zeal of the Lord of hosts will perform this.

Micah 5:2 "But you, Bethlehem Ephrathah, *though* you are little among the thousands of Judah, *yet* out of you shall come forth to Me the One to be Ruler in Israel, whose goings forth *are* from of old, from everlasting."

Luke 2:10-11 Then the angel said to them, "Do not be afraid, for behold, I bring you good tidings of great joy which will be to all people." — "For there is born to you this day in the city of David a Savior, who is Christ the Lord."

Jesus Christ - His Advent

The coming of Jesus is not mentioned in the Koran.

Matthew 1:21-23 "And she shall bring forth a Son, and you shall call His name Jesus, for He will save His people from their sins." — So all this was done that it might be fulfilled which was spoken by the Lord through the prophet, saying: .... *"Behold, the virgin shall be with child, and bear a Son, and they shall call His name Immanuel,"* which is translated, "God with us."

Jesus' Authority

Hebrews 1:1-3   God, who at sundry times and in divers manners spake in time past unto the fathers by the prophets. — Hath in these last days spoken unto us by *his* Son, whom he hath appointed heir of all things, by whom also he made the worlds; — Who being the brightness of *his* glory, and the express image of his person, and upholding all things by the word of his power, when he had by himself purged our sins, sat down on the right hand of the majesty on high;

Jesus' Authority

Sura 5:75   *Christ, the son of Mary, was no more that a messenger;* many were the messengers that passed away before him. His mother was a woman of truth. They had both to eat their (daily) food. See how Allah doth make his Signs clear to them; Yet see in what ways they are deluded away from the truth.

Jesus Christ - Born Again

John 1:12-13   "But as many as received Him, to them He gave the right to become children of God, to those who believe in His name: — Who were born, not of blood, nor of the will of the flesh, nor of the will of man, but of God."

John 3:3   "Jesus answered and said to him, "Most assuredly, I say to you, unless one is born again, he

Jesus - *Born Again*

Jesus can not forgive sins through God, His Father. He is not the Son of God. He is only a messenger equal to the other prophets. All of Jesus' claims to being the Son of God, believing on Him for everlasting life and that He was crucified, shed His blood for the forgiveness of sins, buried, resurrected and now sits at the right hand of God and He will send the cannot see the kingdom of God."

John 3:36 "He who believes in the Son has everlasting life; and he who does not believe the Son shall not see life, but the wrath of God abides on him."

II Corinthians 5:17 "Therefore, if anyone *is* in Christ, *he is* a new creation; old things have passed away; behold, all things have become new."

Jesus' Crucifixion and Resurrection

Matthew 27:35 And they crucified him, and parted his garments, casting lots: that it might be fulfilled which was spoken by the prophet, They parted my garments among them and upon my vesture did they cast lots. (*See* **Mark 15:25; Luke 23:33; John 19:18**)

Luke 24:36, 39 Now as they said these things, Jesus Himself stood in the midst of them, and said unto them, "Peace to you — Behold My hands and My feet, that it is I myself. Handle Me and see, for a spirit does not have flesh and bones as you see I have."

I Corinthians 15:3-4 "For I have delivered to you first of all that which I also received: that Christ died for our sins according to the Scriptures, — And that He was buried, and that He rose again the

Holy Spirit, as a Comforter are all lies purposefully put forth in the Bible.

Jesus' Crucifixion - Resurrection

Sura 4:157 That they said (in boast), "We killed Christ Jesus, the son of Mary, the messenger of Allah," but *they killed him not, nor crucified him, but so it was made to appear to them,* and those who differ therein are full of doubts, with no (certain) knowledge, but only conjecture to follow, for *of a surety they killed him not.*

third day according to the Scriptures."

Jesus' Deity
Not a prophet.

Isaiah 53:5-6 "But He was wounded for our transgressions, he *was* bruised for our iniquities. The chastisement for our peace was upon Him, and by His stripes we are healed. — All we like sheep have gone astray; we have turned, every one, to his own way; and the Lord has laid on Him the iniquity of us all."

Matthew 16:16 And Simon Peter answered and said, Thou art the Christ, the son of the living God. (*See* **John 8:19; John 10-30.**)

Luke 22:19-20 And He took bread, gave thanks and broke *it*, and gave *it* to them, saying, "This is My body which is given for you; do this in remembrance of Me." — Likewise he also took the cup after supper, saying, "This cup *is* the new covenant in My blood, which is shed for you."

Colossians 1:14 "In whom we have redemption through His blood, the forgiveness of sins."

I Peter 2:24 "Who Himself bore our sins in His own body on the tree, that we, having died to sins, might live for righteousness-by whose stripes you were healed."

Jesus' Deity
Only a Phophet.

Sura 2:136 Say ye: "We believe in Allah, and the revelation given to us, and to Abraham, Isma'il, Isaac, Jacob, and the Tribes, and that given to Moses and Jesus, and that given to (all) Prophets from their Lord: We make no difference between one and another of them: and we submit to Allah.

Sura 9:30 The Jews call "Uzayr a son of God," and the Christians call "Christ the Son of God." *That is a saying from their mouth;* (In this) they but imitate what the Unbelievers of old used to say. Allah's curse be on them: how they are deluded away from the Truth!

Jesus' Miracles

John 2:11 This beginning of miracles did Jesus in Cana of Galilee, and manifested forth his glory; and his disciples believed on him.

Jesus Christ - *Son of God*

NB: In the New Testament Jesus' name appears 968 times; Christ appears 558 times; and He is referred to as the Son of God or God as His Father 49 times.

John 3:16 "For God so loved the world, that he gave his only begotten Son, that whosoever believeth in him should not perish, but have everlasting life."

John 10:30 "I and *My* Father are one."

John 14:6 "Jesus said to him, "I am the way, the truth, and the life. No one comes to the Father except through Me."

Hebrews 5:5 So also Christ glorified not himself to be made an high priest; but he that said unto him,

Jesus' Miracles

Sura 3:49 And (appoint him) a messenger to the Children of Israel (with this message): "I have come to you, with a Sign from your Lord, in that *I make for you out of clay, as it were, the figure of a bird, and breathe into it, and it becomes a bird by Allah's leave:* And I heal those born blind, and the lepers, and I quicken the dead, by Allah's leave; And I declare to you what ye eat, and what ye store in your houses. Surely therein is a Sign for you if ye did believe.

Jesus - *Not Son of God*

Sura 4:171 O People of the Book! Commit no excesses in your religion: nor say of Allah aught but the truth. Christ Jesus the son of Mary was (no more than) a Messenger of Allah, and his word, which he bestowed on Mary, and a spirit proceeding from him: so believe in Allah and his Messengers. Say not "Three": desist: it will be better for you: for Allah is one God: glory be to Him: (far exalted is he) above having a son. To Him belong all things in the heavens and on earth. And enough is Allah as a disposer of affairs.

Thou are my Son, to-day have I begotten thee.

I John 5:1 Whosoever believeth that Jesus is the Christ is born of God: and every one that loveth him that begat loveth him also that is begotten of him.

Jews - *From the Tribe of Judah, One of Twelve Tribes of the Hebrew Children*

After King Solomon's death his Kingdom was divided into the Northern Kingdom 'The House of Israel', with its' capitol in Samaria, and the Southern Kingdom, 'The House of Judah', with its' capitol in Jerusalem. Between 496 & 470 BC, Nebuchadnezzar defeated the Southern Kingdom and took the people to Babylon as captives. In 425 BC King Cyrus, King of Persia, who had gained control of Babylon, financed their return to Jerusalem to rebuild the temple. At that time they became known as Jews.

Jews

Sura 3:69-72 It is the wish of a section of the People of the Book to lead you astray. But they shall lead you astray (not you), but themselves, and they do not perceive! — Ye People of the Book! Why reject ye the signs of Allah, of which ye are (yourselves) witnesses? — Ye People of the Book! Why do ye clothe truth with falsehood, and conceal the truth, while ye have knowledge? — A section of the People of the Book say: "Believe in the morning what is revealed to the believers, but reject it at the end of the day: perchance they may (themselves) turn back;

Sura 3:98-99 Say: "O People of the Book! Why reject ye the signs of Allah, when Allah is Himself witness to all ye do?" — Say: "O ye People of the Book! Why obstruct ye those who believe from the path of Allah, seeking to make it crooked, while ye were yourselves witnesses (to Allah's Covenant)? But Allah is not unmindful of all that ye do."

Sura 4:154-161 And for their Covenant we raised over them the Mount (Sinai); and (on another occasion) we said: "Enter the gate with humility"; and (once again) we commanded them: "Transgress not in the matter of the Sabbath." And we took from them a solemn Covenant. — (They have incurred divine displeasure): in that they broke their Covenant; that they rejected the signs of Allah; that they slew the Messengers in defiance of right; that they said, "Our hearts are the wrappings"; nay Allah hath set the seal on their hearts for their blasphemy, and little is it they believe; — That they rejected faith; that they uttered against Mary a grave false charge; — That they said (in boast), "We killed Christ Jesus the son of Mary, the Messenger of Allah"; but they killed him not, nor crucified him. Only a likeness of that was shown to them. And those who differ therein are full of doubts, with no (certain) knowledge. But only conjecture to follow, for of a surety they killed him not: — Nay, Allah raised him up unto Himself; and Allah is exalted in power, wise; — And there is none of the People of the Book but must believe in Him before his death; and on the day of judgment He will be a witness against them; — For the iniquity of the Jews we made unlawful for them certain (foods) good and wholesome which had been lawful for them; and that they hindered many from Allah's way; — That they took usury, though they were forbidden; and that they devoured men's wealth wrongfully; - we have prepared for those among them who reject faith a grievous chastisement.

Sura 5:51 O ye who believe! Take not the Jews And the Christians for your friends and protectors: they are but friends and protectors to each other. And he amongst you that turns to them (for friendship) is of them. Verily Allah guideth not a people unjust.

Jihad

The New Testament of the Bible was written 500 years before the Koran and Jihad is not mentioned, but the spirit of the Jihad (Holy War) is diametrically opposite to that of the Bible.

Jihad - *Fighting, Striving*
(*See War*)

Sura 2:216 Fighting is prescribed upon you, and ye dislike it. But it is possible that ye dislike a thing which is good for you, and that ye love a thing which is bad for you. But Allah knoweth, and ye know not.

Sura 2:218 Those who believed and those who suffered exile and fought (and stove and struggled) in the path of Allah, - they have the hope of the mercy of Allah: and Allah is oft-forgiving, most merciful.

Sura 3:139-140 So lose not heart, Nor fall into despair: for ye must gain mastery if ye are true in faith.

— If a wound hath touched you, be sure a similar wound hath touched the others. ...

Sura 3:142 Did ye think that ye would enter Heaven without Allah testing those of you who fought hard (in His cause) and remained steadfast?

Sura 4-95 Not equal are those believers who sit (at home), except those who are disabled. And those who strive and fight in the cause of Allah with their goods and their persons. Allah hath granted a grade higher to those who strive and fight with their goods and persons than to those who sit (at home). Unto all (in faith) hath Allah promised good: but those who strive and fight hath He distinguished above those who sit (at home) by a great reward.

Sura 5:35 O ye who believe! Do your duty to Allah, seek the means of approach unto Him, and strive (with might and main) in His cause: that ye may prosper.

Sura 5:54 O ye who believe! If any from among you turn back from his faith, soon will Allah produce a people whom He will love as they will love Him, - lowly with the believers, mighty against the rejecters, fighting in the way of Allah, and never afraid of the reproaches of such as find fault.

That is the grace of Allah, which He will bestow on whom He pleaseth. And Allah encompasseth all, and he knoweth all things.

Sura 8:74 Those who believe, and emigrate, and fight for the faith, in the cause of Allah, as well as those who give (them) asylum and aid, - these are (all) in very truth the believers: for them is the forgiveness of sins and a provision most generous.

Sura 9:19-20 Do ye consider the giving of drink to pilgrims, or the maintenance of the Sacred Mosque, equal to (the pious service of) those who believe in Allah and the Last Day, and strive with might and main in the cause of Allah? They are not equal in the sight of Allah: and Allah guides not those who do wrong.

Sura 9:24 Say: if it be that your fathers, your sons, your brothers, your mates, or your kindred: the wealth that ye have gained; the commerce in which ye fear a decline: or the dwellings in which ye delight - are dearer to you than Allah or His Messenger, or the striving in His cause; - then wait until Allah brings about His decision: and Allah guides not the rebellious.

Sura 9:44 Those who believe in Allah and the Last Day ask thee for no exemption from fighting with their goods and persons. And Allah knoweth well those who do their duty.

Sura 9:73 O Prophet! strive hard against the unbelievers and the hypocrites, and be firm against them. Their abode is Hell, - an evil refuge indeed.

Sura 9:86-89 When a Sura comes down, enjoining them to believe in Allah and to strive and fight along with His Messenger, those with wealth and influence among them ask thee for exemption, and say: "Leave us (behind): we would be with those who sit (at home)". — They prefer to be with (the women), who remain behind (at home): their hearts are sealed and so they understand not. — But the Messenger, and those who believe with him, strive and fight with their wealth and their persons: for them are (all) good things: and it is they who will prosper. — Allah hath prepared for them gardens under which rivers flow, to dwell therein: that is the supreme triumph!

Sura 29:6 And if any strive (with might and main), they do so for their own souls: for Allah is free of all needs from all creation.

Sura 29:69 And those who strive in our (cause), - we will certainly guide them to our paths: for verily Allah is with those who do right.

Sura 49:15 Only those are believers who have believed in Allah and His Messenger, and have never since doubted, but have striven with their belongings and their persons in the cause of Allah: such are the sincere ones.

Jinns

The New Testament of the Bible was written 500 years before the Koran and Jinns is not mentioned. The concept of another creature, other than mankind, is not found in the Bible.

Jinns - *Made for Hell*

Sura 6:128 On the day when He will gather them all together, (and say): "O ye assembly of Jinns much (toll) did ye take of men." Their friends amongst men will say: "Our Lord! we made profit from each other: but (alas!) we reached our term - which Thou didst appoint for us." He will say: "The fire be your dwelling-place: you will dwell therein for ever, except as Allah willeth." For thy Lord is full of wisdom and knowledge.

Sura 6:130 "O ye assembly of Jinns and men! came there not unto you Messengers from amongst you, setting forth unto you my signs, and warning you of the meeting of this day of yours?" They will say: "We bear witness against ourselves." It was the life of this world that deceived them. So against themselves will they bear witness that they rejected faith.

Sura 7:179 Many are the Jinns and men we have made for Hell:

they have hearts wherewith they understand not, eyes wherewith they see not, and ears wherewith they hear not. They are like cattle, - nay more misguided: for they are heedless (of warning).

Sura 11:119 Except those on whom thy Lord hath bestowed His mercy: and for this did He create them: and the word of thy Lord shall be fulfilled: "I will fill Hell with Jinns and men all together."

Sura 15:27 And the Jinn race, we had created before, from the fire of a scorching wind.

Sura 18:50 Behold! We said to the angels, "Prostrate to Adam": they prostrated except Iblis. He was one of the Jinns, and he broke the command of his Lord will ye then take him and his progeny as protectors rather than Me? And they are enemies to you! Evil would be the exchange for the wrong-doers.

Sura 51:56 I have only created Jinns and men, that they may serve Me.

Sura 55:14-15 He created man from sounding clay like unto pottery, — And He created Jinns from the fire free of smoke:

Judgment Day
Last Days referred to more than 300 times.

Judgment Day
Referred to more than 150 times in the Koran.

Isaiah 2:2-4 And it shall come to pass in the last days, *that* the mountain of the Lord's house shall be established in the top of the mountains, and shall be exalted above the hills; and all nations shall flow unto it. — And many people shall go and say, Come ye, and let us go up to the mountain of the Lord, to the house of the God of Jacob; and he will teach us of his ways, and we will walk in his paths: for out of Zion shall go forth the law, and the word of the Lord from Jerusalem. — And he shall judge among the nations, and shall rebuke many people: and they shall beat their swords into plowshares, and their spears into pruninghooks: nation shall not lift up sword against nation, neither shall they learn war any more.

Zechariah 12:9 And it shall come to pass in that day, *that* I will seek to destroy all the nations that come against Jerusalem.

I John 4:17 Herein is our love made perfect, that we may have boldness in the day of judgment: because as he is, so are we in this world.

II Peter 2:9 The Lord knoweth how to deliver the godly out of temptations, and to reserve the unjust unto the day of judgment to be punished:

Sura 39:67-75 No just estimate have they made of Allah, such as is due to Him: on the Day of Judgment the whole of the earth will be but His handful, and the heavens will be rolled up in His right hand: Glory to Him! High is He above the partners the attribute to Him! — The trumpet will (just) be sounded, when all that are in the heavens and on earth will swoon, except such as it will please Allah (to exempt). Then will a second one be sounded, when, behold, they will be standing and looking on! — And the Earth will shine with the light of its Lord: the record (of deeds) will be placed (open); the prophets and the witnesses will be brought forward; and a just decision pronounced between them; and they will not be wronged (in the least). — And to every soul will be paid in full (the fruit) of its deeds; and (Allah) knoweth best all that they do. — The unbelievers will be led to Hell in groups: until, when they arrive there, its gates will be opened. And its keepers will say, "Did not messengers come to you from among yourselves, rehearsing to you the signs of your Lord, and warning you of the meeting of this day of yours?" The answer will be: "True: but the decree of chastisement has been proved true against the unbelievers!" — (To them) will be said: "Enter ye the gates of Hell, to dwell therein: and evil is (this) abode of the arrogant!" — And those who

62

II Peter 3:7 But the heavens and the earth, which are now, by the same word are kept in store, reserved unto fire against the day of judgment and perdition of ungodly men.

feared their Lord will be led to the Gardens in groups: until behold, they arrive there; its gates will be opened; and its keepers will say: "Peace be upon you! Enter ye here to dwell therein." — They will say: "Praise be to Allah, who has truly fulfilled His promise to us, and has give us (this) land in heritage: we can dwell in the Garden as we will: how excellent a reward for those who work (righteousness)!" — And thou wilt see the angels surrounding the throne (divine) on all sides, singing glory and praise to their Lord. The decision between them (at Judgment) will be in (perfect) justice, and the cry (on all sides) will be, "Praise be to Allah, the Lord of the Worlds!"

Sura 78:17-25 Verily the day of sorting out is a thing appointed, - The day that the trumpet shall be sounded, and ye shall come forth in crowds; - And the heavens shall be opened as if there were doors, - And the mountains shall vanish, as if they were a mirage. - Truly Hell is as a place of ambush - For the transgressors a place of destination: - They will dwell therein for ages. - Nothing cool shall they taste therein, nor any drink, - Save a boiling fluid and a fluid, dark, murky, intensely cold,

Koran

There is no mention of the Koran in the Bible. The Koran was

Koran - *More Important Than the Bible*

Sura 42:52 And thus have we, by

written more than 500 years after the Bible.

our command, sent inspiration to thee: thou knewest not (before) what was revelation, and what was faith; but we have made the (Quran) a light, wherewith we guide such of our servants as we will; and verily thou dost guide (men) to the straight way,

Sura 43:2-4 By the book that makes things clear, — We have made it a Quran in Arabic that ye may be able to understand. — And verily, it is in the mother of the book, with us, high (in dignity), full of wisdom.

Love

I John 4:19-21 We love him, because he first loved us. — If a man say, I love God, and hateth his brother, he is a liar: for he that loveth not his brother whom he hath seen, how can he love God whom he hath not seen? — And this commandment have we from him, That he who loveth God love his brother also.

I John 5:1-3 Whosoever believeth that Jesus is the Christ is born of God: and every one that loveth him that begat loveth him also that is begotten of him. — By this we know that we love the children of God, when we love God, and keep his commandments. — For this is the love of God, that we keep his commandments: and his commandments are not grievous.

Love

The concept of loving one's neighbor be he enemy or friend is not taught in the Koran. One can trust his friend (a believer) but should have nothing to do with the unbeliever. (See Enemies, Unbelievers and War.)

Sura 60:1 O ye who believe! Take not My enemies and yours as friends (or protectors), - offering them (your) love, even though they have rejected the truth that has come to you, and have (on the contrary) driven out the Messenger and yourselves (from your homes), (simply) because ye believe in Allah your Lord! If ye have come out to strive in My way and to seek My good pleasure, showing friendship unto them in secret: for I know full well all that ye conceal and all that ye reveal. And any of you that

Romans 13:8-10 Owe no man any thing, but to love one another: for he that loveth another hath fulfilled the law. — For this, Thou shalt not commit adultery, Thou shalt not kill, Thou shalt not steal, Thou shalt not bear false witness, Thou shalt not covet; and if *there be* any other commandment, it is briefly comprehended in this saying, namely, Thou shalt love thy neighbour as thyself. — Love worketh no ill to his neighbour: therefore love *is* the fulfilling of the law.

Mary - *Mother of Jesus*
Virgin birth is referred to more than 25 times in the Old and New Testaments.

Luke 1:27, 30-35 "...and the virgin's name was Mary. — And the angel said unto her, Fear not, Mary: for thou hast found favour with God. — thou shalt conceive in they womb, and bring forth a son, and shalt call his name Jesus. — He shall be great, and shall be called the Son of the Highest: and the Lord God shall give unto him the throne of his father David: — And he shall reign over the house of Jacob for ever; and of his kingdom there shall be no end. — said Mary unto the angel, How shall this be, seeing I know not a man? — And the angel answered and said unto her, The Holy Ghost shall come upon thee, and the power of the Highest shall over-

does this has strayed from the straight path.

Mary - *Mother of Jesus*
Sura 19: 16-35 Relate in the Book (the story of) Mary, when she withdrew from her family to a place in the East. — She placed a screen (to screen herself) from them: then we sent to her our angel, and he appeared before her as a man in all respects. — She said "I seek refuge from thee to (Allah) most gracious: (come not near) if thou dost fear Allah." — He said: "Nay, I am only a messenger from thy Lord (to announce) to thee the gift of a pure son." — She said: "How shall I have a son, seeing that no man has touched me, and I am not unchaste?" — He said: "So (it will be): thy Lord saith, 'That is easy for Me; and (we wish) to appoint him as a sign unto men and a mercy from us': it is a matter (so) decreed," — So she conceived him, and she retired with him to a remote place. — And the pains of

shadow thee: therefore also that holy thing which shall be born of thee shall be called the Son of God."

Matthew 1: 18, 20, 21, 25... "Now the birth of Jesus Christ was on this wise: When as his mother Mary was espoused to Joseph, before they came together, she was found with child of the Holy Ghost. — fear not to take unto thee Mary thy wife: for that which is conceived in her is of the Holy Ghost. — and thou shalt call his name Jesus: for he shall save his people from their sins. — And knew her not till she had brought forth her firstborn son: and he called his name Jesus."

childbirth drove her to the trunk of a palm-tree: She cried (in her anguish): "Ah, would that I had died before this! would that I have been a thing forgotten. — But (a voice) cried to her from beneath the (palm-tree): "Grieve not! for thy Lord hath provided a rivulet beneath thee; — "And shake towards thyself the trunk of the palm-tree; it will let fall fresh ripe dates upon thee. — "So eat and drink and cool (thine) eye. And if thou dost see any man, say, 'I have vowed a fast to (Allah) most gracious, and this day will I enter into no talk with any human being'" — At length she brought the (babe) to her people, carrying him (in her arms), they said: "O Mary! Truly a strange thing has thou brought! — "O sister of Aaron! Thy father was not a man of evil, nor thy mother a woman unchaste!" — But she pointed to the babe. They said: "How can we talk to one who is a child in the cradle?" — He said: "I am indeed a servant of Allah: He hath given me revelation and made me a prophet: — "And He hath made me blessed wheresoever I be, and hath enjoined on me prayer and zakat as long as I live; — "(He hath made me) kind to my mother, and not overbearing or unblest; — "So peace is on me the day I was born, the day that I die, and the day that I shall be raised up to life (again)" — Such (was) Jesus the son of Mary: (it is) a statement of truth, about which they (vainly) dispute. — It is not befitting to (the majesty of) Allah that he should beget a son. Glory be to Him! When He determines a matter, He only says to it, "Be", and it is.

Mecca - Islam's Holy City and Site of the Ka'bah

Mecca is not mentioned in the Bible. God's holy city is Jerusalem.

Mecca - *First House of Worship - the Kabah*

Sura 3: 96-97 The first House (of worship) appointed for men was that at Bakka: full of blessing and of guidance for all the worlds. — In it are signs manifest; the Station of Abraham; whoever enters it attains security; pilgrimage thereto is a duty men owe to Allah, - those who can afford the journey; but if any deny faith, Allah stands not in need of any of His creatures.

Moon - *Calendar*

In the Bible all dates and prophecies use the sun for timing and not the moon.

Moon - *Calendar*

Sura 2:189 They ask thee concerning the new moons. Say: They are but signs to mark fixed periods of time in (the affairs of) men. And for pilgrimage. It is no virtue if ye enter your houses from the back: it is virtue if ye fear Allah. Enter houses through the proper doors: And fear Allah: that ye may prosper.

Sura 10:5 It is He who made the sun to be a shining glory and the moon to be a light (of beauty), and measured out stages for it, that ye might know the number of years and the count (of time). Nowise did Allah create this but in truth and righteousness. (Thus) doth He explain His signs in detail, for those who know.

Moses - *Birth*

Exodus 2:1-10 And there went a man of the house of Levi, and took to *wife* a daughter of Levi. — And the woman conceived, and bare a son: and when she saw him that he was a goodly *child,* she hid him three months. — And when she could not longer hide him, she took for him an ark of bulrushes, and daubed it with slime and with pitch, and put the child therein; and she laid *it* in the flags by the river's brink. — And his sister stood afar off, to wit what would be done to him. — And the daughter of Pharaoh came down to wash *herself* at the river; and her maidens walked along by the river's side; and when she saw the ark among the flags, she sent her maid to fetch it. — And when she had opened it, she saw the child: and, behold the babe wept. And she had compassion on him, and said, This is *one* of the Hebrews' children. — Then said his sister to Pharaoh's daughter, Shall I go and call to thee a nurse of the Hebrew women, that she may nurse the child for thee? — And Pharaoh's daughter said to her, Go. And the maid went and called the child's mother. — And Pharaoh's daughter said unto her, Take this child away, and nurse it

Moses - *Birth*

Sura 28:8-9 Then the people of Pharaoh picked him up (from the river): (It was intended) that (Moses) should be to them an adversary and a cause of sorrow: For Pharaoh and Haman and (all) their hosts were men of sin. *The wife of Pharaoh* said: "(Here is) a joy of the eye, for me and for thee: slay him not. It may be that he will be of use to us, or we may adopt him as a son." And they perceived not (what they were doing).

for me, and I will give *thee* thy wages. And the woman took the child, and nursed it. — And the child grew, and she brought him unto Pharaoh's daughter, and he became her son. And she called his name Moses: and she said, Because I drew him out of the water.

Moses - *With Pharaoh*

The complete account of Moses with Pharaoh can be found in **Exodus Chapters 3** through **12.** *It is different from the Koran.*

Moses - *With Pharaoh*

Sura 7:104-123 Moses said: "O Pharaoh! I am a Messenger from the Lord of the Worlds, — One for whom it is right to say nothing but truth about Allah. Now have I come unto you (people), from your Lord with a clear (sign): So let the Children of Israel depart along with me." — (Pharaoh) said: "If indeed thou hast come with a sign, show it forth, - if thou tellest the truth." — Then (Moses) threw his rod, and behold! it was a serpent, plain (for all to see)! — And he drew out his hand, and behold! It was white to all beholders! — Said the chiefs of the people of Pharaoh: "This is indeed a sorcerer well-versed." — "His plan is to get you out of your land: then what is it ye counsel?" — They said: "Keep him and his brother in suspense (for a while); and send to the cities men to collect. — And bring up to thee all (our) sorcerers well-versed." — So there came the sorcerers to Pharaoh: They said, "Of course we shall have a (suitable) reward if we win!" — He said: "Yea, (and more), - for ye shall in that case be (raised

to posts) nearest (to my person)."
— They said: "O Moses! Wilt thou
throw (first), or shall we have the
(first) throw?" — Said Moses:
"Throw ye (first)." So when they
threw, they bewitched the eyes of
the people, and struck terror into
them: and they showed a great
(feat of) magic. — We revealed to
Moses "Throw thy rod": and
behold! It swallow up all the falsehoods which they fake! — Thus
truth was confirmed. And all that
they did was made of no effect. —
So they were vanquished there and
then, and turned about humble. —
But the sorcerers fell down prostrate in adoration. — Saying: "We
believe In the Lord of the Worlds.
— "The Lord of Moses and
Aaron." — Said Pharaoh: "Believe
ye in Him before I give you per-
mission? Surely this is a trick which
ye have planned in the city to drive
out its people: But soon shall ye
know (the consequences)." (*See
sura 7:124-137 and 10:75-90 for
accounts different from the
Bible*).

Sura 20:9-24 Was the story of
Moses reached thee? — Behold, he
saw a fire: so he said to his family,
"Tarry ye; I perceive a fire; perhaps
I can bring you some burning
brand therefrom or find some
guidance at the fire." — But when
he came to the fire, He was called
"O Moses! — Verily I am thy Lord!
therefore put off thy shoes: thou art

in the sacred valley Tuwa. — "I have chosen thee: listen, then to the inspiration (given to thee). — "Verily, I am Allah: there is no god but I; so serve thou Me (only), and establish regular prayer for my remembrance. — "Verily the hour is coming - I have almost kept it hidden - for every soul to receive its reward by the measure of its endeavour. — "Therefore let not such as believe not therein but follow their own lusts, divert thee therefrom, lest thou perish!"... — "And what is that in thy right hand, O Moses?" — He said, "It is my rod: on it I lean; with it I beat down fodder for my flocks; and in it I find other uses." — (Allah) said, "Throw it, O Moses!" — He threw it, and behold! It was a snake, active in motion. — (Allah) said, "Seize it, and fear not: we shall return it at once to its former condition"... — "Now draw they hand close to thy side: It shall come forth white (and shining), without harm (or strain), - as another sign, — "In order that we may show thee of our greater signs. — Go thou to Pharaoh, for he has indeed transgressed all bounds."

Sura 28:34-42 "And my brother Aaron - he is more eloquent in speech than I: so send him with me as a helper, to confirm (and strengthen) me: for I fear that they may accuse me of falsehood." — He said: "We will certainly

71

strengthen thy arm through thy brother, and invest you both with authority, so they shall not be able to touch you: with our signs shall ye triumph, - you two as well as those who follow you." — When Moses came to them with our clear signs, they said: "This is nothing but sorcery faked up: never did we hear the like among our fathers of old!" — Moses said: "My Lord knows best who it is that comes with guidance from Him and whose end will be best in the hereafter: certain it is that the wrong-doers will not prosper." — Pharaoh said: "O Chiefs! no god do I know for you but myself: therefore, O Haman! light me a (kiln to bake bricks) out of clay, and build me a lofty palace, that I may mount up to the god of Moses: But as far as I am concerned, I think (Moses) is a liar!" — And he was arrogant and insolent in the land, beyond reason, - he and his hosts: they thought that they would not have to return to us!" — So we seized him and his hosts, and we flung them into the sea: Now behold what was the end of those who did wrong! — And we made them (but) leaders inviting to the fire; and on the Day of Judgment no help shall they find. — In this world we made a curse to follow them: and on the Day of Judgment they will be among the loathed (and despised).

Moses - *On the Mount*

Exodus 19:3-20 And Moses went up unto God, and the Lord called unto him out of the mountain, saying, Thus shalt thou say to the house of Jacob, and tell the children of Israel; — Ye have seen what I did unto the Egyptians, and *how* I bare you on eagles' wings, and brought you unto myself. — Now therefore, if ye will obey my voice indeed, and keep my covenant, then ye shall be a peculiar treasure unto me above all people: for all the earth is mine: — And ye shall be unto me a kingdom of priests, and an holy nation. These *are* the words which thou shalt speak unto the children of Israel. — And Moses came and called for the elders of the people, and laid before their faces all these words which the Lord commanded him. — And all the people answered together, and said, All that the Lord hath spoken we will do. — And Moses returned the words of the people unto the Lord. — And the Lord said unto Moses, Lo, I come unto thee in a thick cloud, that the people may hear when I speak with thee and believe thee for ever. And Moses told the words of the people unto the Lord. — And the Lord said unto Moses, Go unto the people, and sanctify them to-day and to-morrow, and let them wash their clothes, — And be ready against the third day: for the third day the Lord will come down in the sight

Moses - *On the Mount*

Sura 7:143-146 (*no mention of the 10 Commandments*) When Moses came to the place appointed by us, and his Lord addressed him, He said: "O my Lord! Show (Thyself) to me, that I may look upon Thee." Allah said: "By no means canst thou see Me (direct; but look upon the mount; if it abide in its place, then shalt thou see Me. When his Lord manifested Himself to the Mount, He made it as dust, And Moses fell down in a swoon. When he recovered his senses he said: "Glory be to Thee! To Thee I turn in repentance, and I am the first to believe." — (Allah) said: "O Moses! I have chosen thee above (other) men, by the messages I (have given thee) and the words I (have spoken to thee); take then the (revelation) which I give thee, and be of those who give thanks." — And we ordained for him in the Tablets in all matters, admonition and explanation of all things, (and said): "Take and hold these with firmness, and enjoin thy people to hold fast by the best in the precepts: Soon shall I show you the homes of the wicked, - (how they lie desolate)." — Those who behave arrogantly on the earth in defiance of right - them will I turn away from my signs: even if they see all the signs, they will not believe in them; and if they see the way of right conduct, they will not adopt it as the way; but if they see

73

of all the people upon mount Sinai. — And thou shalt set bounds unto the people round about, saying, Take heed to yourselves, that ye go *not* up into the mount, or touch the border of it: whosoever toucheth the mount shall be surely put to death: — There shall not an hand touch it, but he shall surely be stoned, or shot through, whether *it be* beast or man, it shall not live: when the trumpet soundeth long, they shall come up to the mount. — And Moses went down from the mount unto the people, and sanctified the people; and they washed their clothes. — And he said unto the people, Be ready against the third day: come not at *your* wives. — And it came to pass on the third day in the morning, that there were thunders and lightnings, and a thick cloud upon the mount, and the voice of the trumpet exceeding loud; so that all the people that was in the camp trembled. — And Moses brought forth the people out of the camp to meet with God; and they stood at the nether part of the mount. — And mount Sinai was altogether on a smoke, because the Lord descended upon it in fire: and the smoke thereof ascended as the smoke of a furnace, and the whole mount quaked greatly. — And when the voice of the trumpet sounded long, and waxed louder and louder, Moses spake, and God answered him by a voice. — And

the way of error, that is the way they will adopt. For they have rejected our signs, and failed To take warning from them.

the Lord came down upon mount Sinai, on the top of the mount: and the Lord called Moses *up* to the top of the mount; and Moses went up. (*See* **Exodus 20:1-17**)

Moses - *Golden Calf*

Exodus 32: 1-6 And when the people saw that Moses delayed to come down out of the mount, the people gathered themselves together unto Aaron, and said unto him, Up, make us gods, which shall go before us; for *as for* this Moses, the man that brought us up out of the land of Egypt, we wot (*know*) not what is become of him. — And Aaron said unto them, Break off the golden earrings, which *are* in the ears of your wives, of your sons, and of your daughters, and bring *them* unto me. — And all the people brake off the golden earrings which were in their ears, and brought *them* unto Aaron. — And he received *them* at their hand, and fashioned it with a graving tool, after he had made it a molten calf: and they said, These *be* thy gods, O Israel, which brought thee up out of the land of Egypt. — And when Aaron saw *it,* he built an altar before it; and Aaron made proclamation, and said, To-morrow *is* a feast to the Lord. — And they rose up early on the morrow, and offered burnt offerings, and brought peace offerings; and the people sat down to eat and to drink and rose up to play.

Moses - *Story of the Golden Calf* (*account #1*)

Sura 7:148-156 The people of Moses made, in his absence, out of their ornaments, the body of a calf, (for worship): having lowing sound did they not see that it could neither speak to them, nor show them the way? They took it for worship and they did wrong. — When they repented, and saw that they had erred, they said: "If our Lord have not mercy upon us and forgive us, we shall indeed be among the losers." — When Moses came back to his people, angry and grieved, he said: "Evil it is that ye have done in my place in my absence: did ye make haste to bring on the judgment of your Lord?" He put down the Tablets, seized his brother by (the hair of) his head, and dragged him to him, Aaron said: "Son of my mother! The people did indeed reckon me as naught, and went near to slaying me! Make not the enemies rejoice over my misfortune, nor count thou me amongst the people of sin." — Moses prayed: "O my Lord! Forgive me and my brother! Admit us to thy mercy! For Thou art the most merciful of those who show mercy!" — Those

Exodus 32:15-16 And Moses turned, and went down from the mount, and the two tables of the testimony *were* in his hand: the tables *were* written on both their sides; on the one side and on the other *were* they written. — And the tables *were* the work of God, and the writing *was* the writing of God, graven upon the tables.

Exodus 32:19-26 And it came to pass, as soon as he came nigh unto the camp, that he saw the calf, and the dancing: and Moses' anger waxed hot, and he cast the tables out of his hands, and brake them beneath the mount. — And he took the calf which they had made, and burnt *it* in the fire, and ground *it* to powder, and strawed *it* upon the water, and made the children of Israel drink *of it.* — And Moses said unto Aaron, What did this people unto thee, that thou has brought so great a sin upon them? — And Aaron said, Let not the anger of my lord wax hot: thou knowest the people, that they *are set* on mischief. — For they said unto me, Make us gods, which shall go before us: for *as for* Moses, the man that brought us up out of the land of Egypt, we wot not what is become of him. — And I said unto them, Whosoever hath any gold, let them break *it* off. So they give *it* me: then I cast it into the fire, and there came out this calf. — And when Moses saw that the

who took the calf (for worship) will indeed be overwhelmed with wrath from their Lord and with shame in this life: Thus do we recompense those who invent (falsehoods). — But those who do wrong but repent thereafter and (truly) believe, - verily thy Lord is thereafter Oft-forgiving, Most Merciful. — When the anger of Moses was appeased, he took up the Tablets: in the writing thereon was guidance and mercy for such as fear their Lord. — And Moses chose seventy of his people for our place of meeting: when they were seized with violent quaking, He prayed: "O my Lord! If it had been thy will Thou couldst have destroyed, long before, both them and me: wouldst Thou destroy us for the deeds of the foolish ones among us? This is no more than thy trial: by it Thou causest whom Thou wilt stray, and Thou leadest whom Thou wilt into the right path. Thou art our protector: So forgive us and give us thy mercy; for Thou art the best of those who forgive. — "And ordain for us that which is good, in this life and in the hereafter: For we have turned unto Thee." He said: "I afflict my punishment on whom I will; but my mercy extendeth to all things. That (mercy) I shall ordain for those who do right, and pay zakat and those who believe in our signs;

people *were* naked; (for Aaron had made them naked unto *their* shame among their enemies:) — Then Moses stood in the gate of the camp, and said, Who *is* on the Lord's side? *let him come* unto me. And all the sons of Levi gathered themselves together unto him.

Exodus 32:31-35 And Moses returned unto the Lord, and said, Oh, this people have sinned a great sin, and have made them gods of gold. — Yet now, if thou wilt forgive their sin; and if not, blot me, I pray thee, out of thy book which thou has written. — And the Lord said unto Moses, Whosoever hath sinned against me, him will I blot out of my book. — Therefore now go, lead the people unto *the place* of which I have spoken unto thee: behold, mine angel shall go before thee: nevertheless in the day when I visit I will visit their sin upon them. — And the Lord plagued the people, because they made the calf, which Aaron made.

Moses - *Story of the Golden Calf* (*account #2*)

Sura 20:86-98 So Moses returned to his people in a state of anger and sorrow. He said: "O my people! did not your Lord make a handsome promise to you? Did then the promise seem to you long (in coming)? Or did ye desire that wrath should descend from your Lord on you, and so ye broke your promise to me?" — They said: "We broke not the promise to thee, as far as lay in our power: but we were made to carry the weight of the ornaments of the (whole) people, and we threw them (into the fire), and that was what the Samiri suggested. — "Then he brought out (of the fire) before the (people) the image of a calf. It seemed to low: So they said: "This is your god, and the god of Moses, but (Moses) has forgotten!" — Could they not see that it could not return them a word (for answer), and that it had no power either to harm them or to do them good? — Aaron had already before this said to them: "O my people! Ye are being tested in this: for verily your Lord is (Allah) most gracious: so follow me and obey my command." — They had said: "We will not cease to worship it, will devote ourselves to it until Moses returns to us." — (Moses) said: "O Aaron! What kept thee back, when thou sawest them going wrong — From following me? Didst thou then disobey my order?" — (Aaron) replied: "O son of my mother! Seize (me) not by my beard nor by (the hair of) my head! Truly I feared lest thou shouldst say, Thou has caused a division among the Children Of Israel, and thou didst not observe my word! — (Moses) said: "What then is thy case, O Samiri?" — He replied: "I saw what they say not: so I took a handful (of dust) from the footprint of the Messenger, and threw it (into the calf): Thus did my soul suggest to me."

Moses - *Raised from the Dead*

Sura 2:55-56 And remember ye said: "O Moses! We shall never believe in thee until we see Allah manifestly," thereupon thunderbolt seize you. — Then we raised you up after your death; ye had the chance to be grateful.

Muhammad

Not mentioned in the Bible, nor is it forecast that another prophet will come after Jesus.

Muhammad - *Can Ask Allah for Your Forgiveness*

Sura 4:64 We sent not a Messenger, but to be obeyed, in accordance with the leave of Allah. If they had only, when they were unjust to themselves, come unto thee and asked Allah's forgiveness. And the Messenger had asked forgiveness for them, they would have found Allah indeed oft-returning, most merciful.

Muhammad - _Equal to Allah_

Sura 4:80 He who obeys the Messenger, obeys Allah: but if any turn away, we have not sent thee to watch over them.

Muhammad - _Prophet of Allah_

Sura 7:157-158 Those who follow the Messenger, the unlettered Prophet, whom they find mentioned in their own (Scriptures), - in the Taurat and the Gospel; - for he commands them what is just and forbids them what is evil; he allows them as lawful what is good (and pure) and prohibits them from what is bad (and impure): he releases them from their heavy burdens and from the yokes that are upon them. So it is those who believe in him, honour him, help him, and follow the light which is sent down with him, - it is they who will prosper." — Say: "O men! I am sent unto you all, as the Messenger of Allah, to whom belongeth the dominion of the heavens and the earth: there is no god but He: it is He that giveth both life and death. So believe in Allah and His Messenger. The unlettered Prophet, who believeth in Allah and His words: follow him that (so) ye may be guided."

Sura 50:1 Qaf: By the glorious Qur-an (Thou art Allah's Messenger).

Noah - Son

Genesis 7:7 And Noah went in, and his sons, and his wife, and his sons' wives with him, into the ark, because of the waters of the flood. (*See* **Gen. 7:1-13**)

Noah - Ark - Flood

Genesis 6:11-14 The earth (*region*) also was corrupt before God, and the earth (*region*) was filled with violence. — And God looked upon the earth (*region*), and, behold, it was corrupt; for all flesh had corrupted his way upon the earth (*region*). — And God said unto Noah, The end of all flesh is come before me; for the earth (*region*) is filled with violence through them; and, behold, I will destroy them with the earth (*region*).

Genesis 8:4 And the ark rested in the seventh month, on the seventeenth day of the month, upon the mountains of Ararat.

Sura 62:2 It is He who has sent amongst the unlettered a messenger from among themselves, to rehearse to them His signs, to purify them, and to instruct them in The Book and wisdom, - although they had been, before, in manifest error;

Noah - *Son*

Sura 11:41-43 So the ark floated with them on the waves (Towering) like mountains, *and Noah called out to his son, who had separated himself (from the rest):*....and the waves came between them and the son was among those overwhelmed in the flood. (*See Sura 11:32-48*)

Noah - *Ark - Flood*

Sura 11:44 Then the word went forth: "O earth! swallow up thy water, and O sky! Withhold (thy rain)!" And the water abated, and the matter was ended. *The ark rested on Mount Judi,* and the word went forth: "Away with those who do wrong!"

Parable of Four Birds

Not mentioned in the Bible.

Parable of Four Birds

Sura 2:260 Behold! Abraham said: "My Lord! Show me how Thou givest life to the dead." He said: "Dost thou not then believe?" He said: "Yea! but to satisfy my own heart." He said: "Take four birds; tie them (cut them into pieces), then put a portion of them: on every hill, and call to them: they will come to thee (flying) with speed. Then know that Allah is exalted in power, wise."

Parable of Giving to Allah

Not mentioned in the Bible.

Parable of Giving to Allah

Sura 2:261-262 The parable of those who spend their wealth in the way of Allah is that of a grain of corn: it groweth seven ears, and each ear hath a hundred grains. Allah giveth manifold increase to whom he pleaseth: and Allah careth for all and he knoweth all things. — Those who spend their wealth in the cause of Allah, and follow not up their gifts with reminders of their generosity or with injury, - for them their reward is with their Lord: on them shall be no fear, nor shall they grieve.

Prisoners of War

Not mentioned in the Bible.

Prisoners of War

Sura 8:67 It is not fitting for a prophet that he should have prisoners of war until he hath thoroughly subdued the land. Ye look for the temporal goods of this world; but Allah looketh to the hereafter: and Allah is exalted in might, wise.

Promised Land

Promised by God to the seed of Abraham, Isaac and Jacob.

Genesis 12:7 And the Lord appeared unto Abram, and said, "Unto thy seed will I give this land: and there builded he an altar unto the Lord, who appeared unto him."

Genesis 15:7 And he said unto him, "I *am* the Lord that brought thee out of Ur of the Chal'dees, to give thee this land to inherit it."

Genesis 28:13 And, behold, the Lord stood above it, and said, "I *am* the Lord God of Abraham thy father, and the God of Isaac: the land whereon thou liest, to thee will I give it and to thy seed;"

Joshua: 1:2-6 "Moses my servant is dead; now therefore arise, go over this Jordan, thou, and all this people, unto the land which I do give to them, *even* to the children of Israel. — Every place that the sole of your foot shall tread upon, that have I given unto you, as I said unto Moses. — From the wilderness and this Lebanon even unto the great river, the river Euphrates, all the land of the Hittites, and unto the great sea toward the going down of the sun, shall be your coast — There shall not any man be able to stand before thee all the days of thy life: as I was with Moses, *so* I will be with thee: I will

Promised Land

No mention that God promised the land to the seed of Abraham, Isaac and Jacob.

not fail thee, nor forsake thee. —
Be strong and of a good courage:
for unto this people shalt thou
divide for an inheritance the land,
which I sware unto their fathers to
give them."

Religion

*No mention that Islam shall prevail
over all other religions.*

Religions - *Prevail Over All*

Sura 9:33 It is He who hath sent
His Messenger with guidance and
the religion of truth, to cause it to
prevail over all religion, even
though the pagans may detest (it).
(*See Islam and Chapter 4 The
Koran.*)

Retaliation

*No mention of retaliation to your
enemies in the New Testament; the
fact is that one should love your
enemies. (see Enemies)*

Retaliation

Sura 3:138-140 Here is a plain
statement to men, a guidance and
instruction to those who fear Allah!
— So lose not heart. Nor fall into
despair: for ye must gain mastery if
ye are true in faith. — If a wound
hath touched you, be sure a similar
wound hath touched the others.
Such days (of varying fortunes) we
give to men and men by turns:
that Allah may know those that
believe, and that he may take to
himself from your ranks martyr-
witnesses (to truth). And Allah
loveth not those that do wrong.

Sura 5:45 We ordained therein for
them: "Life for life, eye for eye,
nose for nose, ear for ear, tooth for
tooth, and wounds equal for
equal." But if any one remits the
retaliation by way of charity, it is an
act of atonement for himself. And

Salvation

Hebrews 5:9 And being made perfect, he became the author of eternal salvation unto all them that obey him; (see Jesus Christ)

Sin

Isaiah 59:2 "But your iniquities have separated you from your God; and your sins have hidden *His* face from you, so that He will not hear."

Romans 3:23 "For all have sinned and fall short of the glory of God."

Romans 5:12 "Therefore, just as through one man sin entered the world, and death through sin, and thus death spread to all men, because all sinned."

Sin - *Forgiveness*

Matthew 6: 9-15 "After this manner therefore pray ye: Our Father which art in heaven, Hallowed be thy name. — Thy kingdom come. Thy will be done in earth, as *it is* in

Salvation

Sura 9:20 Those who believe, and emigrate and strive with might and main, in Allah's cause, with their goods and their person, have the highest rank in the sight of Allah: they are the people who will achieve (salvation).

Sin

Sura 4:64 We sent not a Messenger, but to be obeyed, in accordance with the leave of Allah. If they had only, when they were unjust to themselves, come unto thee and asked Allah's forgiveness. And the Messenger had asked forgiveness for them, they would have found Allah indeed oft-returning, most merciful.

Sura 4:111-112 And if any one earns sin, he earns it against his own soul: for Allah is full of knowledge and wisdom. — But if any one earns a fault or a sin and throws it on to one that is innocent, he carries (on himself) (both) a false charge and a flagrant sin.

Sin - *Forgiveness*

Sura 4:110 If any one does evil or wrongs his own soul but afterwards seeks Allah's forgiveness, he will find Allah oft-forgiving, most merciful.

heaven. — Give us this day our daily bread. — And forgive us our debts, as we forgive our debtors. — And lead us not into temptation, but deliver us from evil: For thine is the kingdom, and the power, and the glory, for ever. Amen. — For if ye forgive men their trespasses, your heavenly Father will also forgive you: — But if ye forgive not men their trespasses, neither will your Father forgive your trespasses."

Matthew 12:31-32 "Wherefore I say unto you, all manner of sin and blasphemy shall be forgiven unto men: but the blasphemy *against* the *Holy* Ghost shall not be forgiven unto men. — And whosoever speaketh a word against the Son of man, it shall be forgiven him: but whosoever speaketh against the Holy Ghost, it shall not be forgiven him, neither in the *world,* neither in the world to come."

Matthew 18:21-22 Then came Peter to him, and said, "Lord, how oft shall my brother sin against me, and I forgive him? till seven times?" — Jesus saith unto him, "I say not unto thee, Until seven times: but, Until seventy times seven."

Matthew 18:35 "So likewise shall my heavenly Father do also unto you, if ye from your hearts forgive not every one his brother their trespasses."

Sura 8:74 Those who believe, and emigrate, and fight for the faith, in the cause of Allah, as well as those who give (them) asylum and aid, - these are (all) in very truth the believers: for them is the forgiveness of sins and a provision most generous.

Sura 61:10-12 O ye who believe! Shall I lead you to a bargain that will save you from a grievous chastisement? — That ye believe in Allah and His Messenger, and that ye strive (your utmost) in the cause of Allah, with your wealth and your persons: that will be best for you, if ye but knew! — He will forgive you your sins, and admit you to gardens beneath which rivers flow, and to beautiful mansions in gardens of eternity: that is indeed the supreme triumph.

Mark 11:25-26 "And when ye stand praying, forgive, if ye have aught against any: that your Father also which is in heaven may forgive you your trespasses. — But if ye do not forgive, neither will your Father which is in heaven forgive your trespasses."

Luke 5:24-25 "But that ye may know that the Son of man hath power upon earth to forgive sins, (he said unto the sick of the palsy,) I say unto thee, 'Arise, and take up they couch, and go into thine house.'" — And immediately he rose up before them, and took up that whereon he lay, and departed to his own house, glorifying God.

Luke 23:33-34 And when they were come to the place, which is called Calvary, there they crucified him, and the malefactors, one on the right hand, and the other on the left. — Then said Jesus, "Father forgive them; for they know not what they do." And they parted his raiment, and cast lots.

I John 1:7-9 But if we walk in the light, as he is in the light, we have fellowship one with another, and the blood of Jesus Christ his Son cleanseth us from all sin. — If we say that we have no sin, we deceive ourselves, and the truth is not in us. — If we confess our sins, he is faithful and just to forgive us our sins, and to cleanse us from all unrighteousness.

Solomon - *Story of the Queen of Sheba*

I Kings 10:1-13 And when the queen of Sheba heard of the fame of Solomon concerning the name of the Lord, she came to prove him with hard questions. — And she came to Jerusalem with a very great train, with camels that bare spices, and very much gold, and precious stones: and when she was come to Solomon, she communed with him of all that was in her heart. — And Solomon told her all her questions: there was not *any* thing hid from the king, which he told her not. — And when the queen of Sheba had seen all Solomon's wisdom, and the house that he had built, — And the meat of his table, and the sitting of his servants, and the attendance of his ministers, and their apparel, and his cupbearers, and his ascent by which he went up unto the house of the Lord; there was no more spirit in her. — And she said to the king," It was a true report that I heard in mine own land of thy acts and of thy wisdom. — Howbeit I believed not the words, until I came, and mine eyes had seen *it:* and, behold the half was not told me: thy wisdom and prosperity exceedeth the fame which I heard. — Happy *are* thy men, happy *are* these thy servants, which stand continually before thee, *and* that hear thy wisdom. — Blessed be the Lord thy God, which delighted in thee, to set thee on the

Solomon - *Story of Queen of Sheba*

Completely different than in the Bible. (*See* **I Kings 10:1-13** and **II Chronicles 9:1-12**)

Sura 27:15:44 We give knowledge to David and Solomon: and they both said: "Praise be to Allah, who has favoured us above many of his servants who believe!" — And Solomon was David's heir. He said: "O ye people! We have been taught the speech of birds, and we have been given of everything this is indeed grace manifest (from Allah)." — And before Solomon were marshalled his hosts, - of Jinns and men and birds, and they were all kept in order and ranks.——At length, when they came to a valley of ants, one of the ants said: "O ye ants, get into your habitations, lest Solomon and his hosts crush you (under foot) without knowing it." — So he smiled, amused at her speech; and he said: "O my Lord! so order me that I may be grateful for thy favours, which thou has bestowed on me and on my parents, and that I may work the righteousness that will please thee: And admit me, by thy grace, to the ranks of thy righteous servants." — And he took a muster of the birds; and he said: "Why is it I see not the Hoopoe? Or is he among the absentees? — I will certainly punish him with severe punishment, or execute him, unless he bring me a throne of Israel: because the Lord loved Israel for ever, therefore made he thee king, to do judgment and justice." — And she gave the king an hundred and twenty talents of gold, and of spices very great store, and precious stones: there came no more such abundance of spices as these which the queen of Sheba gave to king Solomon. — And the navy also of Hiram, that brought gold from Ophir, brought in from Ophir great plenty of almug trees, and precious stones.

II Chronicles 9:1-12 And when the queen of Sheba heard of the fame of Solomon, she came to prove Solomon with hard questions at Jerusalem, with a very great company, and camels that bare spices, and gold in abundance, and precious stones: and when she was come to Solomon, she communed with him of all that was in her heart. — And Solomon told her all her questions: and there was nothing hid from Solomon which he told her not. — And when the queen of Sheba had seen the wisdom of Solomon, and the house that he had built, — And the meat of his table, and the sitting of his servants, and the attendance of his ministers, and their apparel; his cupbearers also, and their apparel; and his ascent by which he went up into the house of the Lord; there was no more spirit in her. — And she said to the

clear reason (for absence)." — But the Hoopoe tarried not far: he (came up and) said: "I have compassed which thou has not compassed, and I have come to thee form Saba with tidings true. — I found (there) a woman ruling over them and provided with every requisite; and she has a magnificent throne. — I found her and her people worshipping the sun besides Allah: Satan has made their deeds seem pleasing in their eyes, and has kept them away from the path, so they receive no guidance, — So that they worship not Allah who brings forth what is hidden in the heavens and the earth, and knows what ye hide and what ye reveal. — Allah! - there is no god but he! - lord of the throne supreme!" — (Solomon) said: "Soon shall we see whether thou has told the truth or lied — Go thou, with this letter of mine, and deliver it to them: then draw back from them, and (wait to) see what answer they return"... — (The Queen) said: "Ye chiefs! here is - delivered to me - a letter worthy of respect. — It is from Solomon, and is (as follows): 'In the name of Allah, most gracious, most merciful: — "'Be ye not arrogant against me, but come to me in submission (to the true religion).'" — She said: "Ye chiefs! Advise me in (this) my affair: no affair have I decided except in your presence." — They said: "We are endued with strength, and given to vehement king, "*It was* a true report which I heard in mine own land of thine acts, and thy wisdom: — Howbeit I believed not their words, until I came, and mine eyes have seen *it:* and, behold, the one half of the greatness of thy wisdom was not told me: *for* thou exceedest the fame that I heard. — Happy *are* thy men, and happy *are* these thy servants, which stand continually before thee, and hear thy wisdom. — Blessed be the Lord thy God, which delighted in thee to set thee on his throne, *to be* king for the Lord thy God: because thy God loved Israel, to establish them for ever, therefore made he thee king over them, to do judgment and justice." — And she gave the king an hundred and twenty talents of gold and of spices great abundance, and precious stones: neither was there any such spice as the queen of Sheba gave king Solomon. — And the servants also of Huram, and the servants of Solomon, which brought gold from Ophir, brought algum trees and precious stones. — And the king made *of* the algum trees terraces to the house of the Lord, and to the king's palace, and harps and psalteries for singers: and there were none such seen before in the land of Judah. — And king Solomon gave to the queen of Sheba all her desire, whatsoever she asked, beside *that* which she had brought unto the king. So she

war: but the command is with thee; so consider what thou will command." — She said: "Kings, when they enter a country, despoil it, and make the noblest of its people its meanest thus do they behave. — But I am going to send him a present, and (wait) to see with what (answer) return (my) ambassadors." — Now when (the embassy) came to Solomon, he said: "Will ye give me abundance in wealth? But that which Allah has given me is better than that which he has given you! Nay it is ye who rejoice in your gift! — Go back to them, and be sure we shall come to them with such hosts as they will never be able to meet: we shall expel them from there in disgrace, and they will feel humbled (indeed)." — He said (to his own men): "Ye Chiefs! which of you can bring me her throne before they come to me in submission?" — A stalwart of the Jinn said: "I will bring it to thee before thou rise from thy council: indeed I have full strength for the purpose, and may be trusted." — Said one who had knowledge of the book: "I will bring it to thee before ever thy glance returns to thee. Then when (Solomon) saw it placed firmly before him, he said: "This is by the grace of my Lord! - to test me whether I am grateful or ungrateful! And if any is grateful, truly his gratitude is (a gain) for his own soul; but if any is ungrateful, truly turned, and went away to her own land, she and her servants."

my Lord is free of all needs, supreme in honour!" — He said: "Disguise her throne. Let us see whether she is guided (to the truth) or is one of those who are not rightly guided." — So when she arrived, she was asked, "Is this thy throne?" She said, "It seems the same. And knowledge was bestowed on us in advance of this, and we have submitted to Allah (in Islam)." — And he diverted her from the worship of others besides Allah: for she was (sprung) of a people that had no faith. — She was asked to enter the lofty palace: but when she saw it, she thought it was a lake of water, and she (tucked up her skirts), uncovering her legs. He said: "This is but a palace paved smooth with slabs of glass," She said: "O my Lord! I have indeed wronged my soul: I do (now) submit (in Islam), with Solomon, to the lord of the worlds."

The Ten Commandments

Exodus 20:1-17 And God spake all these words, saying, — I *am* the Lord thy God, which have brought thee out of the land of Egypt, out of the house of bondage. — Thou shalt have no other gods before me. — Thou shalt not make unto thee any graven image, or any likeness of *any thing* that is in heaven above, or that is in earth beneath, or that is in the water under the earth: — Thou shalt not bow down thyself to them, nor serve them: for I the

The Ten Commandments

No mention of the specific Ten Commandments or of Moses receiving them on mount Sinai.

Lord thy God *am* a jealous God, visiting the iniquity of the fathers upon the children unto the third and fourth *generation* of them that hate me; — And shewing mercy unto thousands of them that love me, and keep my commandments. — Thou shalt not take the name of the Lord thy God in vain; for the Lord will not hold him guiltless that taketh his name in vain. — Remember the sabbath day, to keep it holy. — Six days shalt thou labour, and do all thy work: — But the seventh day *is* the sabbath of the Lord thy God: *in it* thou shalt not do any work, thou, nor thy son, nor thy daughter, thy man-servant, nor thy maidservant, nor thy cattle, nor thy stranger that *is* within thy gates: — For *in* six days the Lord made heaven and earth, the sea, and all that in them *is*, and rested the seventh day: wherefore the Lord blessed the sabbath day, and hallowed it. — Honour thy father and thy mother: that thy days may be long upon the land which the Lord thy God giveth thee. — Thou shalt not kill. — Thou shalt not commit adultery. — Thou shalt not steal. — Thou shalt not bear false witness against thy neighbour. — Thou shalt not covet thy neighbour's house, thou shalt not covet thy neighbour's wife, nor his manservant, nor his maidservant, nor his ox, nor his ass, nor anything that is thy neigh-bour's."

Exodus 32:15-19 And Moses turned, and went down from the mount, and the two tables of the testimony *were* in his hand: the tables *were* written on both their sides: on the one side and on the other *were* they written. — And the tables were the work of God, and the writing was the writing of God, graven upon the tables. — And when Joshua heard the noise of the people as they shouted, he said unto Moses, "*there is* a noise of war in the camp." — "And he said, "*it is* not the voice of *them that* shout for mastery, neither *is it* the voice of *them that* cry for being overcome: *but* the noise of *them that* sing do I hear." — And it came to pass, as soon as he came nigh unto the camp, that he saw the calf, and the dancing: and Moses' anger waxed hot, and he cast the tables out of his hands, and brake them beneath the mount.

Trinity

Although the word 'Trinity' does not appear in the Bible there are many references to the coming of the Holy Spirit or the Comforter. Reference to the Holy Spirit appears more than 100 times in the Bible.

John 14:16-17 "And I will pray the Father, and he shall give you another Comforter (*Holy Spirit*), that he may abide with you for ever; — *Even* the Spirit of truth; whom the world cannot receive,

Trinity

Non-existent

Sura 4:171 O People of the Book! Commit no excesses in your religion: nor say of Allah aught but the truth. Christ Jesus the son of Mary was (no more than) a Messenger of Allah, and His word which he bestowed on Mary, and a spirit proceeding from him: so believe in Allah and his Messengers. Say not "Three": desist: it will be better for you: for Allah is one God: glory be to Him:

because it seeth him not, neither knoweth him: buy ye know him; for he dwelleth with you, and shall be in you."

John 14:26 "But the Comforter (*Holy Spirit*), which is the Holy Ghost, whom the Father will send in my name, he shall teach you all things, and bring all things to your remembrance, whatsoever I have said unto you."

John 15:26 "But when the Comforter (*Holy Spirit*) is come, whom I will send unto you from the Father, even the Spirit of truth, which proceedeth from the Father, he shall testify of me:"

John 16:7 "Nevertheless I tell you the truth; It is expedient for you that I go away: for if I go not away, the Comforter (*Holy Spirit*) will not come unto you; but if I depart, I will send him unto you."

John 7:39 (But this spake he of the Spirit, which they that believe on him should receive: for the holy Ghost was not yet given; because that Jesus was not yet glorified.)

I Corinthians 2:13-14 Which things also we speak, not in the words which man's wisdom tea-cheth; but which the Holy Ghost teacheth; comparing spiritual things with spiritual. — But the natural man receiveth not the

(far exalted is he) above having a son. To Him belong all things in the heavens and on earth. And enough is Allah as a disposer of affairs.

Sura 5:73 They disbelieve who say: Allah is one of three (in a Trinity:) for there is no god except one God. If they desist not from their word (of blasphemy), verily a grievous chastisement will befall the disbelievers. Among them.

things of the Spirit of God: for they are foolishness unto him: neither can he know *them,* because they are spiritually discerned.

I Corinthians 12:3 Wherefore I give you to understand, that no man speaking by the Spirit of God calleth Jesus accursed: and that no man can say that Jesus is the Lord, but by the Holy Ghost.

II Corinthians 13:14 The grace of the Lord Jesus Christ, and the love of God, and the communion of the Holy Ghost, *be* with you all. Amen.

I John 5:7 For there are three that bear record in heaven, the Father, the Word, and the Holy ghost: and these three are one.

I John 5:10 He that believeth on the Son of God hath the witness in himself: he that believeth not God hath made him a liar; because he believeth not the record that God gave of his Son.

Unbelievers
NB: No mention to slay them.

II Corinthians 6:14-18 Be ye not unequally yoked together with unbelievers: for what fellowship hath righteousness with unrighteousness? and what communion hath light with darkness? — And what concord hath Christ with

Unbelievers
(See Enemies)

Sura 4:74-76 Let those fight in the cause of Allah who sell the life of this world for the hereafter. To him who fighteth in the cause of Allah, - whether he is slain or gets victory - soon shall we give him a reward of great (value). — And

94

Belial? or what part hath he that believeth with an infidel?—And what agreement hath the temple of God with idols? for ye are the temple of the living God; as God hath said, I will dwell in them, and walk in *them;* and I will be their God, and they shall be my people. — Wherefore come out from among them, and be ye separate, saith the Lord, and touch not the unclean thing; and I will receive you, — And will be a Father unto you, and ye shall be my sons and daughters, saith the Lord Almighty. *Quoted from* Isaiah 52:11.

Titus 1:15-16 Unto the pure all things are pure: but unto them that are defiled and unbelieving *is* nothing pure; but even their mind and conscience is defiled. — They profess that they know God; but in works they deny him, being abominable, and disobedient, and unto every good work reprobate.

Revelations 21:8 But the fearful, and unbelieving, and the abominable, and murderers, and whoremongers, and sorcerers, and idolaters, and all liars, shall have their part in the lake which burneth with fire and brimstone: which is the second death.

why should ye not fight in the cause of Allah and of those who, being weak, are ill-treated (and oppressed)? - men, women, and children, whose cry is: "Our Lord! Rescue us from this town. Whose people are oppressors; and raise for us from Thee one who will protect; and raise for us from Thee one who will help!" — Those who believe fight in the cause of Allah, and those who reject faith fight in the cause of evil (Tagut): so fight ye against the friends, of Satan: feeble indeed is the cunning of Satan.

Sura 4:89 They but wish that ye should reject faith, as they do, and thus be on the same footing (as they): so take not friends from their ranks until they flee in the way of Allah (from what is forbidden). But if they turn renegades, seize them and slay them wherever ye find them; and (in any case) take no friends or helpers from their ranks:

Sura 4:91 Others you will find that wish to be secure from you as well as that of their people: every time they are sent back to temptation, they succumb thereto: if they withdraw not from you nor give you (guarantees) of peace besides restraining their hands, seize them and slay them wherever ye get them: in their case we have provided you with a clear argument against them.

Sura 5:51 O ye who believe! Take not the Jews And the Christians for your friends and protectors. They are but protectors to each other. And he amongst you that turns to them (for friendship) is of them. Verily Allah guideth not a people unjust.

Sura 8:65-69 O Prophet! rouse the believers to the fight. If there are twenty amongst you, patient and persevering, they will vanquish two hundred: if a hundred. They will vanquish a thousand of the unbelievers: for these are people without understanding. — For the present, Allah hath lightened your (burden), for He knoweth that there is a weak spot in you: but (even so), if there are a hundred of you, patient and persevering, they will vanquish two hundred, and if a thousand, they will vanquish two thousand, with the leave of Allah: for Allah is with those who patiently persevere. — It is not fitting for a Prophet that he should have prisoners of war until he hath thoroughly subdued the land. Ye look for the temporal goods of this world; but Allah looketh to the hereafter: and Allah is exalted in might, wise. — Had it not been for a previous ordainment from Allah, a severe punishment would have reached you for the (ransom) that ye took. — But (now) enjoy what ye took in war, lawful and good: But fear Allah: for Allah is oft-forgiving, most merciful. (*See sura 8 for actions of war*)

Sura 9:5 But when the forbidden months are past, then fight and slay the pagans wherever ye find them, and seize them, beleaguer them, and lie in wait for them in every stratagem (of war); but if they repent, and establish regular prayers. And pay zakat (*alms*) then open the way for them: for Allah is oft-forgiving, most merciful.

Sura 9:73 O Prophet! Strive hard against the unbelievers and the hypocrites, and be firm against them. Their abode is Hell, - an evil refuge indeed.

Sura 98:1-8 Those who disbelieve, among the People of the Book and among the Polytheists (*Christians and pagans*), were not going to depart (from their ways) until there should come to them clear evidence, — Messenger from Allah, rehearsing scriptures kept pure and holy: — Wherein are books right and straight. — Nor did the People of the Book make schisms, until after there came to them clear evidence. — And they have been commanded no more than this: to worship Allah, offering Him sincere devotion, being true (in faith); to establish regular prayer; and to give zakat (alms); and this is the religion right and straight. — Those who disbelieve, among the

People of the Book and among the Polytheists (*Trinity*), will be in hell-fire, to dwell therein (for aye). They are the worst of creatures. — Those who have faith and do righteous deeds, - they are the best of creatures. — Their reward is with Allah: gardens of eternity, beneath which rivers flow; they will dwell therein for ever; Allah well pleased with them, and they with him: all this for such as fear their Lord and cherisher.

Vengeance
Belongs to the Lord not man.

Deuteronomy 32:35 To me *belongeth* vengeance, and recompence; their foot shall slide in *due* time: for the day of their calamity *is* at hand, and the things that shall come upon them make haste.

Psalms 94:1 O Lord God, to whom vengeance belongeth; O God, to whom vengeance belongeth, shew thyself.

Romans 12:19 Dearly beloved, avenge not yourselves, but *rather* give place unto wrath: for it is written, Vengeance is mine; I will repay, saith the Lord.

War - the Battle of Armageddon
For events leading to the battle see Daniel, Chapters 11 & 12; Matthew, Chapter 24; **Mark,**

Vengeance - *Take Revenge*
Sura 3:139-140 So lose not heart. Nor fall into despair: for ye must gain mastery if ye are true in faith. — If a wound hath touched you, be sure a similar wound hath touched the others. Such days (of varying fortunes) we give to men and men by turns; that Allah may know those that believe, and that He may take to Himself from your ranks martyr-witnesses (to truth). And Allah loveth not those that do wrong.

Sura 42:39 And those who, when an oppressive wrong is inflicted on them, (are not cowed but) help and defend themselves.

War - *Against Allah*
Sura 5:33 The punishment of those who wage war against Allah and his Messenger, and strive with might and main for mischief

Chapter 13; Luke Chapter 21; Revelation, Chapters 11 through 19.

Revelation 16:16 And he gathered them together in a place called in the Hebrew tongue Armageddon.

Revelation 19:19 And I saw the beast, and the kings of the earth, and their armies, gathered together to make war against him that sat on the horse, and against his army.

War - *Physical*

In the Old Testament war was sanctioned by God for the Children of Israel to drive out the pagans who occupied the land that God had promised to Abraham, Isaac and Jacob (**Numbers, Deuteronomy, Joshua, Judges, II Samuel, I & II Kings,** and I and **II Chronicles**).

Nowhere in the Bible does God permit the Children of Israel to occupy or obtain, by war, any land other than that promised by God Himself. Strict instructions were given that they should drive out the pagans and not to take their daughters in marriage, nor to worship their gods. They were a separate people. Nowhere in the Old Testament do the Children of Israel invade their neighbors' land.

War - Spiritual

Physical war against your neighbor is far from the teaching of Christ, and

through the land is: execution, or crucifixion, or the cutting off of hands and feet from opposite sides, or exile from the land: that is their disgrace in this world, and a heavy punishment is theirs in the hereafter;

War - *Allah Be With You*

Sura 8:65-69 O Prophet! rouse the believers to the fight. If there are twenty amongst you, patient and persevering, they will vanquish two hundred: if a hundred. They will vanquish a thousand of the unbelievers: for these are a people without understanding. — For the present Allah hath lightened your (burden), for He knoweth that there is a weak spot in you: but (even so), if there are a hundred of you, patient and persevering, they will vanquish two hundred, and if a thousand, they will vanquish two thousand, with the leave of Allah: for Allah is with those who patiently persevere — It is not fitting for a prophet that he should have prisoners of war until he hath thoroughly subdued the land. Ye look for the temporal goods of this world; but Allah looketh to the hereafter: and Allah is exalted in might, wise. — Had it not been for a previous ordainment from Allah, a severe punishment would have reached you for the (ransom) that ye took. — But (now) enjoy what ye took in war, lawful and good: but fear *not discussed in the New Testament. Spiritual war is, however, a reality since the Christian is continually fighting evil powers and the principalities of the earth.*

Romans 8:31-39 What shall we then say to these things? If God *be* for us, who *can* be against us? — He that spared not his own Son, but delivered him up for us all, how shall he not with him also freely give us all things? — Who shall lay any thing to the charge of God's elect? *It is* God that justifieth. — Who is he that condemneth? *It is* Christ that died, yea rather, that is risen again, who is even at the right hand of God, who also maketh intercession for us. — Who shall separate us from the love of Christ? *shall* tribulation, or distress, or persecution, or famine, or nakedness, or peril, or sword? — As it is written, For thy sake we are killed all the day long; we are accounted as sheep for the slaughter. — Nay, in all these things we are more than conquerors through him that loved us. — For I am persuaded, that neither death, nor life, nor angels, nor principalities, nor powers, nor things present, nor things to come, — Nor height, nor depth, nor any other creature, shall be able to separate us from the love of God, which is in Christ Jesus our Lord.

Allah: for Allah Is oft-forgiving, most merciful.

War - *Fight in Cause of Allah*

Sura 4:119-121 "I will mislead them, and I will create in them false desires; I will order them to slit the ears of cattle, and to deface the (fair) nature created by Allah," Whoever, forsaking Allah, takes Satan for a friend, hath of a surety suffered a loss that is manifest. — Satan makes them promises, and creates in them false hopes, but Satan's promises are nothing but deception. — They (his dupes) will have their dwelling in Hell, and from it they will find no way of escape.

War - *If Out Numbered*

Sura 8:65-69 O Prophet! rouse the believers to the fight. If there are twenty amongst you, patient and persevering, they will vanquish two hundred: if a hundred. They will vanquish a thousand of the unbelievers: for these are people without understanding. — For the present, Allah hath lightened your (burden), for He knoweth that there is a weak spot in you: but (even so), if there are a hundred of you, patient and persevering, they will vanquish two hundred, and if a thousand, they will vanquish two thousand, with the leave of Allah: for Allah is with those who patiently persevere. — It is not fitting for

Ephesians 4:1-3 I therefore, the prisoner of the Lord, beseech you that ye walk worthy of the vocation wherewith ye are called, — With all lowliness and meekness, with longsuffering, forbearing one another in love — Endeavouring to keep the unity of the Spirit in the bond of peace.

Ephesians 5:1-2 Be ye therefore followers of God, as dear children; — And walk in love, as Christ also hath loved us, and hath given himself for us an offering and a sacrifice to God for a sweet-smelling savour.

Ephesians 6:10-18 Finally, my brethren, be strong in the Lord, and in the power of his might. — Put on the whole armour of God, that ye may be able to stand against the wiles of the devil. — For we wrestle not against flesh and blood, but against principalities, against powers, against the rulers of the darkness of this world, against spiritual wickedness in high *places.* — Wherefore take unto you the whole armour of God, that ye may be able to withstand in the evil day, and having done all, to stand. — Stand therefore, having your loins girt about with truth, and having on the breastplate of righteousness; — And your feet shod with the preparation of the gospel of peace; — Above all, taking the shield of faith, wherewith ye shall be able to quench all the fiery darts of the

a Prophet that he should have prisoners of war until he hath thoroughly subdued the land. Ye look for the temporal goods of this world; but Allah looketh to the hereafter: and Allah is exalted in might, wise. — Had is not been for a previous ordainment from Allah, a severe punishment would have reached you for the (ransom) that ye took. — But (now) enjoy what ye took in war, lawful and good: but fear Allah: for Allah is oft-forgiving, most merciful.

Sura 9:38-42 O ye who believe! what is the matter with you, that, when ye are asked to go forth in the cause of Allah, ye cling heavily to the earth? Do ye prefer the life of this world to the hereafter? But little is the comfort of this life, as compared with the hereafter. — Unless ye go forth, he will punish you with a grievous penalty, and put others in your place; but Him ye would not harm in the least, for Allah hath power over all things. — If ye help not (the Prophet), (it is no matter): for Allah did indeed help him, when the unbelievers drove him out: being the second of the two they two were in the cave, and he said to his companion, "Have no fear, for Allah is with us": then Allah sent down His peace upon him, and strengthened him with forces which ye saw not, and humbled to the depths the word of the unbelievers. But the word of wicked. — And take the helmet of salvation, and the sword of the Spirit, which is the word of God: — Praying always with all prayer and supplication in the Spirit, and watching thereunto with all perseverance and supplication for all saints;

Allah is exalted to the heights; for Allah is exalted in might, wise. — Go ye forth (whether equipped) lightly or heavily, and strive and struggle, with your goods and your persons, in the cause of Allah. That is best for you, if ye (but knew). — If there had been immediate gain (in sight), and the journey easy, they would (all) without doubt have followed thee, but the distance was long, (and weighed) on them. They would indeed swear by Allah, "If we only could, we should certainly have come out with you:" they would destroy their own souls; for Allah doth know that they are certainly lying.

War - *Reward for Those Who Fight*

Sura 4:95 Not equal are those believers who sit (at home), except those who are disabled. And those who strive and fight in the cause of Allah with their goods and their persons. Allah hath granted a grade higher to those who strive and fight with their goods and persons than to those who sit (at home). Unto all (in faith) hath Allah promised good: but those who strive and fight hath he distinguished above those who sit (at home) by a great reward.

War - *Sacrifice Your Lives in War*

Sura 4:66 If we had ordered them

to sacrifice their lives or to leave their homes, very few of them would have done it: but if they had done what they were (actually) told, it would have been best for them, and would have gone farthest to strengthen their (faith);

Sura 4:74 Let those fight in the cause of Allah who sell the life of this world for the hereafter. To him who fighteth in the cause of Allah, - whether he is slain or gets victory - soon shall we give him a reward of great (value).

Wives

Ephesians 5:25-28 Husbands, love your wives, even as Christ also loved the church, and gave himself for it; — That he might sanctify and cleanse it with the washing of water by the word, — That he might present it to himself a glorious church, not having spot, or wrinkle, or any such thing; but that it should be holy and without blemish — So ought men to love their wives as their own bodies. He that loveth his wife loveth himself.

I Peter 3:7 Likewise, ye husbands, dwell with *them* according to knowledge, giving honour unto the wife, as unto the weaker vessel, and as being heirs together of the grace of life; that your prayers be not hindered.

Wives

Sura 4:34 Men are the protectors and maintainers of women, because Allah has given the one more (strength) than the other, and because they support them from their means. Therefore the righteous women are devoutly obedient, and guard in (the husband's) absence what Allah would have them guard. As to those women on whose part ye fear disloyalty and ill-conduct, *admonish them (first), (next), refuse to share their beds, (and last) beat them (lightly);* * but if they return to obedience, seek not against them means (of annoyance): for Allah is Most High, Most Great (above you all).
The Arabic text, does not include the word 'lightly'. It was added by the translator.

103

Wives - _Polygamy_

Permitted in the Old Testament and stopped approximately 1000 AD. The New Testament permits only one wife.

I Corinthians 7:2 Nevertheless, to _avoid_ fornication, let every man have his own wife, and let every woman have her own husband.

Ephesians 5:20-33 Giving thanks always for all things unto God and the Father in the name of our Lord Jesus Christ; — Submitting yourselves one to another in the fear of God. — Wives, submit yourselves unto your own husbands, as unto the Lord. — For the husband is the head of the wife, even as Christ is the head of the church: and he is the saviour of the body. — Therefore as the church is subject unto Christ, so _let_ the wives _be_ to their own husbands in every thing. — Husbands, love your wives, even as Christ also loved the church, and gave himself for it; — That he might sanctify and cleanse it with the washing of water by the word, — That he might present it to himself a glorious church, not having spot, or wrinkle, or any such thing; but that it should be holy and without blemish. — So ought men to love their wives as their own bodies. He that loveth his wife loveth himself. — For no man ever yet hated his own flesh; but nourisheth and cherisheth it, even as the

Sura 2:223 Your wives are as a tilth* unto you so approach your tilth when or how you will; but do some good act for your souls before hand; and fear Allah, and know that ye are to meet Him (in the Hereafter), and give (these) good tidings to those who believe. *A tilth is a piece of farmland.*

Wives - _Justice Between Wives_

Sura 4:129-130 Ye are never able to do justice between wives even if it is your ardent desire: but turn not away (from a woman) altogether, so as to leave her (as it were) hanging (in the air). If ye come to a friendly understanding, and practise self-restraint, Allah is oft-forgiving, most merciful. — But if they separate Allah will provide abundance for each of them from His all-reaching bounty: for Allah is He that careth for all and is wise.

Wives - _Men to Have Four Wives_

Sura 4:3 If ye fear that ye shall not be able to deal justly with the orphans, marry women of your choice, two, or three, or four; but if ye fear that ye shall not be able to deal justly (with them), then only one, or that which your right hands possess. That will be more suitable, to prevent you from doing injustice.

Lord the church: — For we are members of his body, of his flesh, and of his bones. — For this cause shall a man leave his father and mother, and shall be joined unto his wife, and they two shall be one flesh. — This is a great mystery: but I speak concerning Christ and the church. — Nevertheless let every one of you in particular so love his wife even as himself; and the wife *see* that she reverence *her* husband.

I Peter 3:7 Husbands, likewise, *dwell with them with understanding, giving honor to the wife,* as to the weaker vessel, and as being heirs together of the grace of life, that your prayers may not be hindered.

Wives - *Taken as Booty in War and as Many as Muhammad Pleases*

Sura 33:50-51 O Prophet! We have made lawful to thee thy wives to whom thou hast paid their dowers; and those whom thy right hand possesses out of the captives of war whom Allah has assigned to thee; and daughters of thy paternal uncles and aunts, and daughters of they maternal uncles and aunts, who migrated with thee; and any believing woman who gives herself to the Prophet if the Prophet wishes to wed her; - this only for thee, and not for the believers (at large); we know what we have appointed for them as to their wives and the captives whom their right hands possess; - in order that there should be no difficulty for thee. And Allah is oft forgiving, most merciful. — Thou mayest defer (the turn of) any of them that thou pleasest, and thou mayest receive any thou pleasest: and there is no blame on thee if thou invite one whose (turn) thou hadst set aside. This were nigher to the cooling of their eyes, the prevention of their grief, and their satisfaction - that of all of them - with that which thou hast to give them: And Allah knows (all) that is in your hearts: and Allah is all-knowing most for-bearing.

Wives - _Treatment of Muhammad's Wives_

Sura 33:53 O ye who believe! Enter not the Prophet's houses, - until leave is give you, - for a meal, (and then) not (so early as) to wait for its preparation: but when ye are invited, enter; and when ye have taken your meal, disperse, without seeking familiar talk. Such (behaviour) annoys the Prophet he is shy to dismiss you, but Allah is not shy (to tell you) the truth. And when ye ask (his ladies) for anything ye want, ask them from before a screen: that makes for greater purity for your hearts and for theirs... .

Wives - _Muhammad's Widows Cannot Remarry_

Sura 33:53-55 ...Nor is it right for you that ye should annoy Allah's Messenger, or that ye should marry his widows after him at any time. Truly such a thing is in Allah's sight an enormity. — Whether ye reveal anything or conceal it, verily Allah has full knowledge of all things. — There is no blame (on those ladies if they appear) before their fathers or their sons, their brothers, or their brothers' sons, or their sisters' sons, or their women, or the (slaves) whom their right hands possess. And, (ladies), fear Allah; for Allah is witness to all things.

Women of the Bible

Exodus 15:20 And Miriam the prophetess, the sister of Aaron, took a timbrel in her hand; and all the women went out after her with timbrels and with dances.

Judges 4:4-9 And Deborah, a prophetess, the wife of Lapidoth, she judged Israel at that time. — And she dwelt under the palm tree of Deborah between Ramah and Beth-el in mount Ephraim: and the children of Israel came up to her for judgment. — And she sent and called Barak the son of Abinoam out of Kedesh-naphtali, and said unto him, Hath not the Lord God of Israel commanded, *saying,* Go and draw toward mount Tabor, and take with thee ten thousand men of the children of Naphtali and the children of Zebulun? — And I will draw unto thee to the river Kishon Sisera, the captain of Jabin's army, with his chariots and his multitude; and I will deliver him into thine hand. — And Barak said unto her, If thou wilt go with me, *then* I will go: but if thou wilt not go with me, then I will not go. — And she said, I will surely go with thee: notwithstanding the journey that thou takest shall not be for thine honour; for the Lord shall sell Sisera into the hand of a woman. And Deborah arose, and went with Barak to Kedesh.

Women

Sura 4:11 Allah (thus) directs you as regards your children's (inheritance): to the male, a portion equal to that of two females: ...

Sura 4:15 If any of your women are guilty of lewdness, take the evidence of four (reliable) witnesses from amongst you against them; and if they testify, confine them to houses until death do claim them, or Allah ordain for them some (other) way.

Sura 4:20 But if ye decide to take one wife in place of another, even if ye had given the latter a whole treasure for dower, take not the least bit of it back: would ye take it by slander and a manifest sin?

Sura 24:31 And say to the believing women that they should lower their gaze and guard their modesty; that they should not display their beauty and ornaments except what (ordinarily) appear thereof; that they should draw their veils over their bosoms and not display their beauty except to their husbands, their fathers, their husbands' fathers, their sons, their husbands' sons, their brothers or their brothers' sons.

Judges 4:18-21 And Jael went out to meet Sisera, and said unto him, "Turn in, my lord, turn in to me; fear not." And when he had turned in unto her into the tent, she covered him with a mantle. — And he said unto her, "Give me, I pray thee, a little water to drink; for I am thirsty." And she opened a bottle of milk, and gave him drink, and covered him. — Again he said unto her, "Stand in the door of the tent, and it shall be, when any man doth come and inquire of thee, and say, Is there any man here? that thou shalt say, No. —" Then Jael Heber's wife took a nail of the tent, and took an hammer in her hand, and went softly unto him, and smote the nail into his temples, and fastened it into the ground: for he was fast asleep and weary. So he died.

II Kings 22:14-15 So Hilkiah the priest, and Ahikam, and Achbor, and Shaphan, and Asahiah, went unto Huldah the prophetess, the wife of Shallum the son of Tikvah, the son of Harhas, keeper of the wardrobe; (now she dwelt in Jerusalem in the college;) and they communed with her. — And she said unto them, Thus saith the Lord God of Israel, Tell the man that sent you to me. - - - - -

Nehemiah 6:14 My God, think thou upon Tobiah and Sanballat according to these their works, and

on the prophetess, Noadiah, and
the rest of the prophets, that would
have put me in fear.

Luke 2:36-37 And there was one
Anna, a prophetess, the daughter of
Phanuel, of the tribe of Aser: she
was of a great age, and had lived
with a husband seven years from
her virginity; — And she *was* a
widow of about fourscore and four
years, which departed not from the
temple, but served *God* with fast-
ings and prayers night and day.

Acts 21:9 And the same man had
four daughters, virgins, which did
prophesy.

Chapter Five

Observations

OBSERVATIONS ON THE FLOOD

The Flood happened in approximately 2350 BC.
(Documented by historical facts and the Bible)
The age of the pyramids was from 2700 BC to 2200 BC approximately
500 years.....350 years before the Flood & 150 years after.
(Documented by historical facts and Archeology.) Therefore the
Pyramids were built before the Flood, during the Flood and after
the Flood.
Egypt is only 500 miles from Mt. Ararat.
Both China and India did not experience a decimation of population in
2350 BC.
(Documented by historical facts and Archeology.)

COULD THE BIBLE BE WRONG ABOUT THE FLOOD?

Let's do a bit of research —

In English, the word EARTH can be interchanged with soil, land, terrain, ground, world, globe, etc. and all would or could be right, providing the circumstance and meaning to be conveyed.

In Genesis, Chapter 6, 7 and 8, we have the account of Noah and the FLOOD. In the original manuscripts two words are used, ADAMAH (Adam) *(ref. Hebrew dictionary, Strong #127)* meaning <u>Country</u>, Earth, <u>Ground</u>, Husband, <u>Region, Area, Land</u>, and 'ERETS' *(Strong #776)* meaning Earth [at large or partitively (a Land)] <u>Country</u>, Field, <u>Ground, Land,</u> Way, Wilderness, or World.

111

The first, ADAMAH was used 7 times as "EARTH" and two times as "GROUND"; the second 'ERETS' was used 32 times, all as "EARTH."

The original translators had no problem to select the word "EARTH" as the proper meaning since there had been over 2000 years of tradition and at least 500 years of Churches, artist's paintings, and other items depicting a world wide FLOOD. Selecting any other word would not have been justified.

It has not been more than 80 years that archeologists have indeed found evidence of a great flood in the region or basin of Mt. Ararat.

.....But, strangely enough, that same evidence has been elusive, in the rest of the world.

CONCLUSION

The original translators did not have the archeological facts nor the historical data in 1611. Any one of the above underlined words (which should have been used) would have labeled the translation irresponsible.

The FLOOD therefore was not WORLD-WIDE but restricted to a region or area. The reason of the FLOOD — will be dealt with in a later observation.

Some Interesting Observations

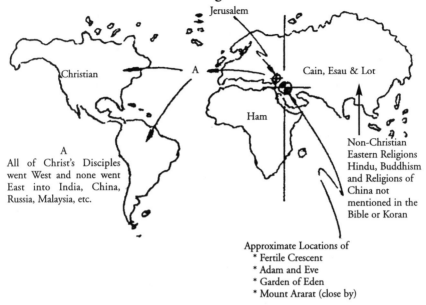

Jerusalem

Christian

A

Cain, Esau & Lot

Ham

A
All of Christ's Disciples
went West and none went
East into India, China,
Russia, Malaysia, etc.

Non-Christian
Eastern Religions
Hindu, Buddhism
and Religions of
China not
mentioned in the
Bible or Koran

Approximate Locations of
* Fertile Crescent
* Adam and Eve
* Garden of Eden
* Mount Ararat (close by)

Cain - Land of Nod
* East of Eden Gen. 4:16
* God put Mark on Cain
   to protect him from other people. Gen. 4:15
   (other people on Earth at that time)
* Genealogy:
Cain Different than Adam
Gen 4:17-24 and Gen 3:1-32
Note: Cain <u>not</u> in Adams

Esau Born <u>Red</u> Gen 25:25
* Sold birthright for red pottage Gen 25:30
* His Name is <u>Edom</u> = Red Ge 25:30
* Generations of Esau (Edom) Gen 36:1-8
* God said "I hated Esau" Mal 1:3 & Rom 9:13
* Esau-Edom-Idumea-Rosh-Russ-Red-
   Russia all the same (Historical fact)
* "The people against whom the Lord hath
   indignation forever" Mal 1:4
* "Thou shall be cut off forever"
   Obediah 1:9, 10 & 18
* Esau married Ishmael's daughter Mahalath
   (Bashemath) Gen 28:9

China
* Chinese legend has it that the first
   Chinese man came from the dragon
   and yellow clay, and his wife from
   Heaven.
* National Emblem is the Dragon
* Less than 1% of all Chinese go to
   Christian Church and even those
   also go to Buddhist. Temple!
* Director of Asian Outreach, Paul E.
   Kauffman in his book "China" Says
   "There is virtually no Chinese
   Christianity."
* "Land of Nod" in Mongolia -
   Northern China (ref. World Book
   Encyclopedia)

OBSERVATIONS ON LINEAGE OF ABRAHAM

APPROXIMATE DATE		REFERENCE

APPROXIMATE DATE		REFERENCE
Pre 4000 BC	Neanderthal — Homo Habilis — Homo Sapien— Homo Sapien-Sapien — Homo Erectus Prestone Age & Stone Age - 6th Day Mankind	Gen 1: 26/27
4000 BC	Adam "God Formed the Man" and Placed Him in the Garden of Eden	Gen 2: 7/8
	And God Gave Adam a Wife (Eve) as a Helpmate	Gen 2: 18-23
	Adam Thru Seth (Not Cain); 9 Generations to Noah	Gen 5: 1-32
2350 BC	Noah - 3 Sons Shem, Ham, & Japheth	Gen 6: 10
(Flood Not World Wide)	Through Shem 8 generations to Abram	Gen 11: 10-26
2000 BC	Abram Borne to Terah	Gen 11: 26
1925 BC	Abram - Left "UR of the Chaldees" - To Haran	Gen 11: 31
	& I (God) Will Make of You a Great Nation	Gen 12: 2
	Abram & Family Left Haran for Canaan	Gen 12: 5
Key	God to Abram "Unto Thy Seed Will I Give This Land" in Gen 28: 3-4	Gen 12: 7 &
	Sarai, Abram's Wife, Was Barren	Gen 16: 1
	& Sarai Suggested That Hagar (From Egypt) Her Hand Maiden, Be Surrogate Mother	Gen 16: 2
1913 BC Key	Abram - Hagar - A Son Ishmael - Angel to Hagar "Your Seed to be	
	Multiplied But He Shall Be a Wildman; His Hand Against Every Man"	Gen 16: 10/12
	"Will I Make a Nation, Because He Is thy Seed" (Note: Singular not Plural)	Gen 21: 13
	Ishmael Mocked & Was Jealous of Isaac (No Love For His Brother)	Gen 21: 9
	Ishmael & Hagar Sent Out From Abraham's Family Because of Family Friction	Gen 21: 14
	God Changes Abram to Abraham & Promises "Seed to Be Kings & Many Nations"	Gen 17: 5/8
	God Changes Sarai to Sarah & Promises Her "Seed to Be Kings & Many Nations"	Gen 17: 15/16
	"My Covenant Will I Establish With Isaac"	Gen 17: 21
1900 BC	Isaac Borne to Sarah (13 Years After Ishmael)	Gen 21: 3
	"In Isaac Shall Thy Seed Be Called"	Gen 21: 12
	I Will Multiply Thy Seed (Isaac) As the Stars of the Heaven, And As the	
	Sand of the Seas; & Thy Seed Shall Possess the Gates of His Enemies	Gen 22: 17
	And in Thy Seed (Isaac) Shall All the Nations of the Earth Be Blessed;	
	Because Thou Hast Obeyed My Voice"	Gen 22: 18

ABRAHAM

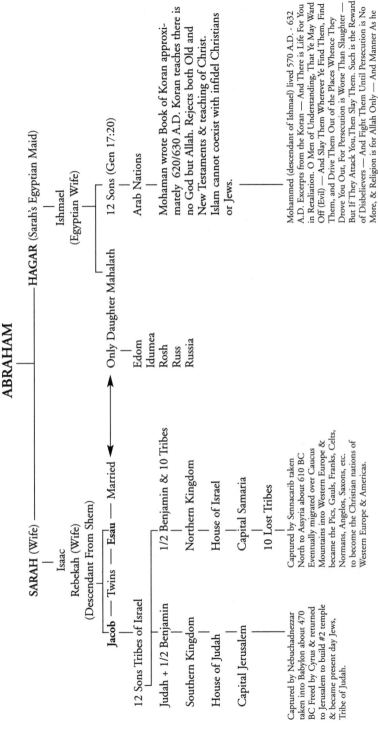

SARAH (Wife) ———————————— **HAGAR** (Sarah's Egyptian Maid)

Isaac

Rebekah (Wife)
(Descendant From Shem)

Ishmael
(Egyptian Wife)

Jacob — Twins — **Esau** — Married —→ Only Daughter Mahalath ←— 12 Sons (Gen 17:20)

12 Sons Tribes of Israel

1/2 Benjamin & 10 Tribes

Edom
Idumea
Rosh
Russ
Russia

Arab Nations

Judah + 1/2 Benjamin

Northern Kingdom

Southern Kingdom

House of Israel

House of Judah

Capital Samaria

Capital Jerusalem

10 Lost Tribes

Mohaman wrote Book of Koran approximately 620/630 A.D. Koran teaches there is no God but Allah. Rejects both Old and New Testaments & teaching of Christ. Islam cannot coexist with infidel Christians or Jews.

Captured by Nebuchadnezzar taken into Babylon about 470 BC Freed by Cyrus & returned to Jerusalem to build #2 temple & became present day Jews, Tribe of Judah.

Captured by Sennacarib taken North to Assyria about 610 BC Eventually migrated over Caucus Mountains into Western Europe & became the Pics, Gauls, Franks, Celts, Normans, Angelos, Saxons, etc. to become the Christian nations of Western Europe & Americas.

Mohammed (descendant of Ishmael) lived 570 A.D. - 632 A.D. Excerpts from the Koran — And There is Life For You in Retaliation. O Men of Understanding, That Ye May Ward Off (Evil) — And Slay Them Wherever Ye Find Them, Find Them, and Drive Them Out of the Places Whence They Drove You Out, For Persecution is Worse Than Slaughter — But If They Attack You, Then Slay Them. Such is the Reward of Disbelievers — And Fight Them Until Persecution is No More, & Religion is for Allah Only — And Manner As he One Who Attacketh You, Attack Him in Like Doeth Unto You. Observe YourDuty to Allah & Know That Allah Is With Those Who Ward Off (Evil).

115

Chapter Six

Where Are We Now?

As we observe violence and terrorism, the need for universal security is increasing each day. World unrest seems at an all time high and the unsolvable problems of the Israeli - Palestinian conflict are becoming more complicated with no end in sight.

Islam is the fastest growing religion in the world today with one of every five being Muslim, about 1.3 billion followers. However, more important is the fact that Islam is a political force and is not compatible with most of the world governments as seen in 'Differences - The Bible versus Koran' (*Chapter 4*) of this book. Allah directs his followers to take a personal revenge of their enemies and not through the court of law. For example, in February, 2002 a band of Muslims attacked a train in India setting it on fire, killing 57 Hindu men, women and children only because they had attended a meeting to build a Hindu temple on a site that had once been a Muslim Mosque.

For an overview of the present world condition, the entire text of the testimony by the Director of Central Intelligence, George J. Tenet, on February 6, 2002, before the Senate Select Committee on Intelligence has been included in this book.

Worldwide Threat - Converging Dangers in a Post 9/11 World
Testimony of Director of Central Intelligence
George J. Tenet
Before The
Senate Select Committee on Intelligence

(as prepared for delivery)

6 February 2002

Mr. Chairman, I appear before you this year under circumstances that are extraordinary and historic for reasons I need not recount. Never before has the subject of this annual threat briefing had more immediate resonance. Never before have the dangers been more clear or more present.

September 11 brought together and brought home – literally – several vital threats to the United States and its interests that we have long been aware of. It is the convergence of these threats that I want to emphasize with you today: the connection between terrorists and other enemies of this country; the weapons of mass destruction they seek to use against us; and the social, economic, and political tensions across the world that they exploit in mobilizing their followers. September 11 demonstrated the dangers that arise when these threats converge – and it reminds us that we overlook at our own peril the impact of crises in remote parts of the world.

This convergence of threats has created the world I will present to you today – a world in which dangers exist not only in those places where we have most often focused our attention, but also in other areas that demand it:

- In places like Somalia, where the absence of a national government has created an environment in which groups sympathetic to Al-Qa'ida have offered terrorists an operational base and potential haven.

- In places like Indonesia, where political instability, separatist and ethnic tensions, and protracted violence are hampering economic recovery and fueling Islamic extremism.

- In places like Colombia, where leftist insurgents who make much of their money from drug trafficking are escalating their assault on the government – further undermining economic prospects and fueling a cycle of violence.

- And finally, Mr. Chairman, in places like Connecticut, where the death of a 94-year-old woman in her own home of anthrax poisoning can arouse our worst fears about what our enemies might try to do to us.

These threats demand our utmost response. The United States has clearly demonstrated since September 11 that it is up to the challenge. But make no mistake: despite the battles we have won in Afghanistan, we remain a nation at war.

TERRORISM

Last year I told you that Usama Bin Ladin and the Al-Qa'ida network were the most immediate and serious threat this country faced. This remains true today despite the progress we have made in Afghanistan and in disrupting the network elsewhere. We assess that Al-Qa'ida and other terrorist groups will continue to plan to attack this country and its interests abroad. Their modus operandi is to have multiple attack plans in the works simultaneously, and to have Al-Qa'ida cells in place to conduct them.

- We know that terrorists have considered attacks in the US against high-profile government or private facilities, famous landmarks, and US infrastructure nodes such as airports, bridges, harbors, and dams. High profile events such as the Olympics or last weekend's Super Bowl also fit the terrorists' interest in striking another blow within the United States that would command worldwide media attention.

- Al-Qa'ida also has plans to strike against US and allied targets in Europe, the Middle East, Africa, and Southeast Asia. American diplomatic and military installations are at high risk – especially in East Africa, Israel, Saudi Arabia, and Turkey.

- Operations against US targets could be launched by Al-Qa'ida cells already in place in major cities in Europe and the Middle East. Al-Qa'ida can also exploit its presence or connections to other groups in such countries as Somalia, Yemen, Indonesia, and the Philippines.

Although the September 11 attacks suggest that Al-Qa'ida and other terrorists will continue to use conventional weapons, one of our highest concerns is their stated readiness to attempt unconventional attacks against us. As early as 1998, Bin Ladin publicly declared that acquiring unconventional weapons was "a religious duty."

- Terrorist groups worldwide have ready access to information on chemical, biological, and even nuclear weapons via the Internet, and we know that Al-Qa'ida was working to acquire some of the most dangerous chemical agents and toxins. Documents recovered from Al-Qa'ida facilities in Afghanistan show that Bin Ladin was pursuing a sophisticated biological weapons research program.

- We also believe that Bin Ladin was seeking to acquire or develop a nuclear device. Al-Qa'ida may be pursuing a radioactive dispersal device – what some call a "dirty bomb."

- Alternatively, Al-Qa'ida or other terrorist groups might also try to launch conventional attacks against the chemical or nuclear industrial infrastructure of the United States to cause widespread toxic or radiological damage.

We are also alert to the possibility of cyber warfare attack by terrorists. September 11 demonstrated our dependence on critical infrastructure systems that rely on electronic and computer networks. Attacks of this nature will become an increasingly viable option for terrorists as they and other foreign adversaries become more familiar with these targets, and the technologies required to attack them.

The terrorist threat goes well beyond Al-Qa'ida. The situation in the Middle East continues to fuel terrorism and anti-US sentiment world-wide. Groups like the Palestine Islamic Jihad (PIJ) and HAMAS have escalated their violence against Israel, and the intifada has rejuvenated once-dormant groups like the Popular Front for the Liberation of Palestine. If these groups feel that US actions are threatening their existence, they may begin targeting Americans directly – as Hizballah's terrorist wing already does.

- The terrorist threat also goes beyond Islamic extremists and the Muslim world. The Revolutionary Armed Forces of Colombia (FARC) poses a serious threat to US interests in Latin America because it associates us with the government it is fighting against.

- The same is true in Turkey, where the Revolutionary People's Liberation Party/Front has publicly criticized the United States and our operations in Afghanistan.

- We are also watching states like Iran and Iraq that continue to support terrorist groups.

- Iran continues to provide support – including arms transfers – to Palestinian rejectionist groups and Hizballah. Tehran has also failed to move decisively against Al-Qa'ida members who have relocated to Iran from Afghanistan.

- Iraq has a long history of supporting terrorists, including giving sanctuary to Abu Nidal.

The war on terrorism has dealt severe blows to Al-Qa'ida and its leadership. The group has been denied its safehaven and strategic command center in Afghanistan. Drawing on both our own assets and increased cooperation from allies around the world, we are uncovering terrorists' plans and breaking up their cells. These efforts have yielded the arrest of nearly 1,000 Al-Qa'ida operatives in over 60 countries, and have disrupted terrorist operations and potential terrorist attacks.

Mr. Chairman, Bin Ladin did not believe that we would invade his sanctuary. He saw the United States as soft, impatient, unprepared, and fearful of a long, bloody war of attrition. He did not count on the fact that we had lined up allies that could help us overcome barriers of terrain and culture. He did not know about the collection and operational initiatives that would allow us to strike – with great accuracy – at the heart of the Taliban and Al-Qa'ida. He underestimated our capabilities, our readiness, and our resolve.

That said, I must repeat that Al-Qa'ida has not yet been destroyed. It and other like-minded groups remain willing and able to strike us. Al-Qa'ida leaders still at large are working to reconstitute the organization and to resume its terrorist operations. We must eradicate these organizations by denying them their sources of financing and eliminating their ability to hijack charitable organizations for their terrorist purposes. We must be prepared for a long war, and we must not falter.

Mr. Chairman, we must also look beyond the immediate danger of terrorist attacks to the conditions that allow terrorism to take root around the world. These conditions are no less threatening to US national security than terrorism itself. The problems that terrorists exploit – poverty, alienation, and ethnic tensions – will grow more acute over the next decade. This will especially be the case in those parts of the world that have served as the most fertile recruiting grounds for Islamic extremist groups.

- We have already seen – in Afghanistan and elsewhere – that domestic unrest and conflict in weak states is one of the factors that create an environment conducive to terrorism.

- More importantly, demographic trends tell us that the world's poorest and most politically unstable regions – which include parts of the Middle East and Sub-Saharan Africa – will have the largest youth populations in the world over the next two decades and beyond. Most of these countries will lack the economic institutions or resources to effectively integrate these youth into society.

THE MUSLIM WORLD

All of these challenges come together in parts of the Muslim world, and let me give you just one example. One of the places where they converge that has the greatest long-term impact on any society is its educational system. Primary and secondary education in parts of the Muslim world is often dominated by an interpretation of Islam that teaches intolerance and hatred. The graduates of these schools – "madrasas" – provide the foot soldiers for many of the Islamic militant groups that operate throughout the Muslim world.

Let me underscore what the President has affirmed: Islam itself is neither an enemy nor a threat to the United States. But the increasing anger toward the West – and toward governments friendly to us – among Islamic extremists and their sympathizers clearly is a threat to us. We have seen – and continue to see – these dynamics play out across the Muslim world. Let me briefly address their manifestation in several key countries.

Our campaign in Afghanistan has made great progress, but the road ahead is fraught with challenges. The Afghan people, with international assistance, are working to overcome a traditionally weak central government, a devastated infrastructure, a grave humanitarian crisis, and ethnic divisions that deepened over the last 20 years of conflict. The next few months will be an especially fragile period.

- Interim authority chief Hamid Karzai will have to play a delicate balancing game domestically. Remaining al Qa'ida fighters in the eastern provinces, and ongoing power struggles among Pashtun leaders there underscore the volatility of tribal and personal relations that Karzai must navigate.

- Taliban elements still at large and remaining pockets of Arab fighters could also threaten the security of those involved in reconstruction and humanitarian operations. Some leaders in the new political order may allow the continuation of opium cultivation to secure advantages against their rivals for power.

123

Let me move next to **Pakistan.** September 11 and the US response to it were the most profound external events for Pakistan since the Soviet invasion of Afghanistan in 1979, and the US response to that. The Musharraf government's alignment with the US – and its abandonment of nearly a decade of support for the Taliban – represent a fundamental political shift with inherent political risks because of the militant Islamic and anti-American sentiments that exist within Pakistan.

President Musharraf's intention to establish a moderate, tolerant Islamic state – as outlined in his 12 January speech – is being welcomed by most Pakistanis, but he will still have to confront major vested interests. The speech is energizing debate across the Muslim world about which vision of Islam is the right one for the future of the Islamic community.

- Musharaff established a clear and forceful distinction between a narrow, intolerant, and conflict-ridden vision of the past and an inclusive, tolerant, and peace-oriented vision of the future.

- The speech also addressed the jihad issue by citing the distinction the Prophet Muhammad made between the "smaller jihad" involving violence and the "greater jihad" that focuses on eliminating poverty and helping the needy.

Although September 11 highlighted the challenges that **India-Pakistan** relations pose for US policy, the attack on the Indian parliament on December 13 was even more destabilizing – resulting as it did in new calls for military action against Pakistan, and subsequent mobilization on both sides. The chance of war between these two nuclear-armed states is higher than at any point since 1971. If India were to conduct large scale offensive operations into Pakistani Kashmir, Pakistan might retaliate with strikes of its own in the belief that its nuclear deterrent would limit the scope of an Indian counterattack.

- Both India and Pakistan are publicly downplaying the risks of nuclear conflict in the current crisis. We are deeply concerned, however, that a conventional war – once begun – could escalate into a nuclear confrontation.

Let me turn now to Iraq. Saddam has responded to our progress in Afghanistan with a political and diplomatic charm offensive to make it appear that Baghdad is becoming more flexible on UN sanctions and inspections issues. Last month he sent Deputy Prime Minister Tariq Aziz to Moscow and Beijing to profess Iraq's new openness to meet its UN obligations and to seek their support.

Baghdad's international isolation is also decreasing as support for the sanctions regime erodes among other states in the region. Saddam has carefully cultivated neighboring states, drawing them into economically dependent relationships in hopes of further undermining their support for the sanctions. The profits he gains from these relationships provide him the means to reward key supporters and, more importantly, to fund his pursuit of WMD. His calculus is never about bettering or helping the Iraqi people.

Let me be clear: Saddam remains a threat. He is determined to thwart UN sanctions, press ahead with weapons of mass destruction, and resurrect the military force he had before the Gulf war. Today, he maintains his vise grip on the levers of power through a pervasive intelligence and security apparatus, and even his reduced military force – which is less than half its pre-war size – remains capable of defeating more poorly armed internal opposition groups and threatening Iraq's neighbors.

As I said earlier, we continue to watch Iraq's involvement in terrorist activities. Baghdad has a long history of supporting terrorism, altering its targets to reflect changing priorities and goals. It has also had contacts with Al-Qa'ida. Their ties may be limited by divergent ideologies, but the two sides' mutual antipathy toward the United States and the Saudi royal family suggests that tactical cooperation between them is possible – even though Saddam is well aware that such activity would carry serious consequences.

In Iran, we are concerned that the reform movement may be losing its momentum. For almost five years, President Khatami and his reformist supporters have been stymied by Supreme Leader Khamenei and the hardliners.

- The hardliners have systematically used the unelected institutions they control – the security forces, the judiciary, and the Guardian's

Council – to block reforms that challenge their entrenched interests. They have closed newspapers, forced members of Khatami's cabinet from office, and arrested those who have dared to speak out against their tactics.

- Discontent with the current domestic situation is widespread and cuts across the social spectrum. Complaints focus on the lack of pluralism and government accountability, social restrictions, and poor economic performance. Frustrations are growing as the populace sees elected institutions such as the Majles and the Presidency unable to break the hardliners' hold on power.

The hardline regime appears secure for now because security forces have easily contained dissenters and arrested potential opposition leaders. No one has emerged to rally reformers into a forceful movement or change, and the Iranian public appears to prefer gradual reform to another revolution. But the equilibrium is fragile and could be upset by a miscalculation by either the reformers or the hardline clerics.

For all of this, reform is not dead. We must remember that the people of Iran have demonstrated in four national elections since 1997 that they want change and have grown disillusioned with the promises of the revolution. Social, intellectual, and political developments are proceeding, civil institutions are growing, and new newspapers open as others are closed.

The initial signs of Tehran's cooperation and common cause with us in Afghanistan are being eclipsed by Iranian efforts to undermine US influence there. While Iran's officials express a shared interest in a stable government in Afghanistan, its security forces appear bent on countering the US presence. This seeming contradiction in behavior reflects deep-seated suspicions among Tehran's clerics that the United States is committed to encircling and overthrowing them – a fear that could quickly erupt in attacks against our interests.

- We have seen little sign of a reduction in Iran's support for terrorism in the past year. Its participation in the attempt to transfer arms to the Palestinian Authority via the Karine-A probably was intended to escalate the violence of the intifada and strengthen the position of Palestinian elements that prefer armed conflict with Israel.

The current conflict between **Israel** and the **Palestinians** has been raging for almost a year and a half, and it continues to deteriorate. The violence has hardened the public's positions on both sides and increased the longstanding animosity between Israeli Prime Minister Sharon and Palestinian leader Arafat. Although many Israelis and Palestinians say they believe that ultimately the conflict can only be resolved through negotiations, the absence of any meaningful security cooperation between Israel and the Palestinian Authority – and the escalating and uncontrolled activities of the Palestine Islamic Jihad and HAMAS – make any progress extremely difficult.

- We are concerned that this environment creates opportunities for any number of players – most notably Iran – to take steps that will result in further escalation of violence by radical Palestinian groups.

- At the same time, the continued violence threatens to weaken the political center in the Arab world, and increases the challenge for our Arab allies to balance their support for us against the demands of their publics.

PROLIFERATION

I turn now to the subject of **proliferation**. I would like to start by drawing your attention to several disturbing trends in this important area. WMD programs are becoming more advanced and effective as they mature, and as countries of concern become more aggressive in pursuing them. This is exacerbated by the diffusion of technology over time – which enables proliferators to draw on the experience of others and to develop more advanced weapons more quickly than they could otherwise. Proliferators are also becoming more self-sufficient. And they are taking advantage of the dual-use nature of WMD - and missile-related technologies to establish advanced production capabilities and to conduct WMD - and missile-related research under the guise of legitimate commercial or scientific activity.

Let me address in turn the primary categories of WMD proliferation, starting with **chemical** and **biological weapons**. The CBW threat continues to grow for a variety of reasons, and to present us with monitoring challenges. The dual-use nature of many CW and BW agents complicates our assessment of offensive programs. Many CW and BW production capabilities are hidden in plants that are virtually indistinguishable from genuine commercial facilities. And the technology behind CW and BW agents is spreading. We assess there is a significant risk within the next few years that we could confront an adversary – either terrorists or a rogue state – who possesses them.

On the **nuclear** side, we are concerned about the possibility of significant nuclear technology transfers going undetected. This reinforces our need to more closely examine emerging nuclear programs for sudden leaps in capability. Factors working against us include the difficulty of monitoring and controlling technology transfers, the emergence of new suppliers to covert nuclear weapons programs, and the possibility of illicitly acquiring fissile material. All of these can shorten timelines and increase the chances of proliferation surprise.

On the missile side, the proliferation of ICBM and cruise missile designs and technology has raised the threat to the US from WMD delivery systems to a critical threshold. As outlined in our recent National Intelligence Estimate on the subject, most Intelligence Community agencies project that by 2015 the US most likely will face ICBM threats from North Korea and Iran, and possibly from Iraq. This is in addition to the longstanding missile forces of Russia and China. Short-and medium-range ballistic missiles pose a significant threat now.

- Several countries of concern are also increasingly interested in acquiring a land-attack cruise missile (LACM) capability. By the end of the decade, LACMs could pose a serious threat to not only our deployed forces, but possibly even the US mainland.

Russian entities continue to provide other countries with technology and expertise applicable to CW, BW, nuclear, and ballistic and cruise missile projects. Russia appears to be the first choice of proliferant states seeking the most advanced technology and training. These sales are a major source of funds for Russian commercial and defense industries and military R&D.

- Russia continues to supply significant assistance on nearly all aspects of Tehran's nuclear program. It is also providing Iran assistance on long-range ballistic missile programs.

Chinese firms remain key suppliers of missile-related technologies to Pakistan, Iran, and several other countries. This is in spite of Beijing's November 2000 missile pledge not to assist in any way countries seeking to develop nuclear-capable ballistic missiles. Most of China's efforts involve solid-propellant ballistic missile development for countries that are largely dependent on Chinese expertise and materials, but it has also sold cruise missiles to countries of concern such as Iran.

- We are closely watching Beijing's compliance with its bilateral commitment in 1996 not to assist unsafeguarded nuclear facilities, and its pledge in 1997 not to provide any new nuclear cooperation to Iran.

- Chinese firms have in the past supplied dual-use CW-related production equipment and technology to Iran. We remain concerned that they may try to circumvent the CW-related export controls that Beijing has promulgated since acceding to the CWC and the nuclear Nonproliferation Treaty.

North Korea continues to export complete ballistic missiles and production capabilities along with related raw materials, components, and expertise. Profits from these sales help P'yongyang to support its missile – and probably other WMD – development programs, and in turn generate new products to offer to its customers – primarily Iran, Libya, Syria, and Egypt. North Korea continues to comply with the terms of the Agreed Framework that are directly related to the freeze on its reactor program, but P'yongyang has warned that it is prepared to walk away from the agreement if it concluded that the United States was not living up to its end of the deal.

Iraq continues to build and expand an infrastructure capable of producing WMD. Baghdad is expanding its civilian chemical industry in ways that could be diverted quickly to CW production. We believe it also maintains an active and capable BW program; Iraq told UNSCOM it had worked with several BW agents.

- We believe Baghdad continues to pursue ballistic missile capabilities that exceed the restrictions imposed by UN resolutions. With substantial foreign assistance, it could flight-test a longer-range ballistic missile within the next five years. It may also have retained the capability to deliver BW or CW agents using modified aircraft or other unmanned aerial vehicles.

- We believe Saddam never abandoned his nuclear weapons program. Iraq retains a significant number of nuclear scientists, program documentation, and probably some dual-use manufacturing infrastructure that could support a reinvigorated nuclear weapons program. Baghdad's access to foreign expertise could support a rejuvenated program, but our major near-term concern is the possibility that Saddam might gain access to fissionable material.

Iran remains a serious concern because of its across-the-board pursuit of WMD and missile capabilities. Tehran may be able to indigenously produce enough fissile material for a nuclear weapon by late this decade. Obtaining material from outside could cut years from this estimate. Iran may also flight-test an ICBM later this decade, using either Russian or North Korean assistance. Having already deployed several types of UAVs – including some in an attack role – Iran may seek to develop or otherwise acquire more sophisticated LACMs. It also continues to pursue dual-use equipment and expertise that could help to expand its BW arsenal, and to maintain a large CW stockpile.

Both **India** and **Pakistan** are working on the doctrine and tactics for more advanced nuclear weapons, producing fissile material, and increasing their nuclear stockpiles. We have continuing concerns that both sides may not be done with nuclear testing. Nor can we rule out the possibility that either country could deploy their most advanced nuclear weapons without additional testing. Both countries also continue development of long-range nuclear-capable ballistic missiles, and plan to field cruise missiles with a land-attack capability.

As I have mentioned in years past, we face several unique challenges in trying to detect WMD acquisition by proliferant states and non-state actors. Their use of denial and deception tactics, and their access to a tremendous amount of information in open sources about WMD production, complicate our efforts. So does their exploitation of space.

The unique spaceborne advantage that the US has enjoyed over the past few decades is eroding as more countries – including China and India – field increasingly sophisticated reconnaissance satellites. Today there are three commercial satellites collecting high-resolution imagery, much of it openly marketed. Foreign military, intelligence, and terrorist organizations are exploiting this – along with commercially available navigation and communications services – to enhance the planning and conduct of their operations.

Let me mention here another danger that is closely related to proliferation: the changing character of warfare itself. As demonstrated by September 11, we increasingly are facing real or potential adversaries whose main goal is to cause the United States pain and suffering, rather than to achieve traditional military objectives. Their inability to match US military power is driving some to invest in "asymmetric" niche capabilities. We must remain alert to indications that our adversaries are pursuing such capabilities against us.

RUSSIA

Mr. Chairman, let me turn now to other areas of the world where the US has key interests, beginning with Russia. The most striking development regarding Russia over the past year has been Moscow's greater engagement with the United States. Even before September 11, President Putin had moved to engage the US as part of a broader effort to integrate Russia more fully into the West, modernize its economy, and regain international status and influence. This strategic shift away from a zero-sum view of relations with the United States is consistent with Putin's stated desire to address the many socioeconomic problems that cloud Russia's future.

During his second year in office, Putin moved strongly to advance his policy agenda. He pushed the Duma to pass key economic legislation on budget reform, legitimizing urban property sales, flattening and simplifying tax rates, and reducing red tape for small businesses. His support for his economic team and its fiscal rigor positioned Russia to pay back wages and pensions to state workers, amass a post-Soviet high of almost $39 billion in reserves, and meet the major foreign debt coming due this year (about $14 billion) and next (about $16 billion).

- He reinvigorated military reform by placing his top lieutenant atop the Defense Ministry and increasing military spending for the second straight year – even as he forced tough decisions on de-emphasizing strategic forces, and pushing for a leaner, better-equipped conventional military force.

This progress is promising, and Putin is trying to build a strong Presidency that can ensure these reforms are implemented across Russia – while managing a fragmented bureaucracy beset by informal networks that serve private interests. In his quest to build a strong state, however, he is trying to establish parameters within which political forces must operate.

This "managed democracy" is illustrated by his continuing moves against independent national television companies.

- On the economic front, Putin will have to take on bank reform, overhaul of Russia's entrenched monopolies, and judicial reform to move the country closer to a Western-style market economy and attract much-needed foreign investment.

Putin has made no headway in Chechnya. Despite his hint in September of a possible dialogue with Chechen moderates, the fighting has intensified in recent months, and thousands of Chechen guerrillas – and their fellow Arab mujahedeen fighters – remain. Moscow seems unwilling to consider the compromises necessary to reach a settlement, while divisions among the Chechens make it hard to find a representative interlocutor. The war, meanwhile, threatens to spill over into neighboring Georgia.

After September 11, Putin emphatically chose to join us in the fight against terrorism. The Kremlin blames Islamic radicalism for the conflict in Chechnya and believes it to be a serious threat to Russia. Moscow sees the US-led counterterrorism effort – particularly the demise of the Taliban regime – as an important gain in countering the radical Islamic threat to Russia and Central Asia.

So far, Putin's outreach to the United States has incurred little political damage, largely because of his strong domestic standing. Recent Russian media polls show his public approval ratings at around 80 percent. The depth of support within key elites, however, is unclear – particularly within the military and security services. Public comments by some senior military officers indicate that elements of the military doubt that the international situation has changed sufficiently to overcome deeply rooted suspicions of US intentions.

Moscow retains fundamental differences with Washington on key issues, and suspicion about US motives persists among Russian conservatives – especially within the military and security services. Putin has called the intended US withdrawal from the ABM treaty a "mistake," but has downplayed its impact on Russia. At the same time, Moscow is likely to pursue a variety of countermeasures and new weapons systems to defeat a deployed US missile defense.

CHINA

I turn next to **China.** Last year I told you that China's drive to become a great power was coming more sharply into focus. The challenge, I said, was that Beijing saw the United States as the primary obstacle to its realization of that goal. This was in spite of the fact that Chinese leaders at the same time judged that they needed to maintain good ties with Washington. A lot has happened in US-China relations over the past year, from the tenseness of the EP-3 episode in April to the positive image of President Bush and Jiang Zemin standing together in Shanghai last fall, highlighting our shared fight against terrorism.

September 11 changed the context of China's approach to us, but it did not change the fundamentals. China is developing an increasingly competitive economy and building a modern military force with the ultimate objective of asserting itself as a great power in East Asia. And although Beijing joined the coalition against terrorism, it remains deeply skeptical of US intentions in Central and South Asia. It fears that we are gaining regional influence at China's expense, and it views our encouragement of a Japanese military role in counterterrorism as support for Japanese rearmament – something the Chinese firmly oppose.

As always, Beijing's approach to the United States must be viewed against the backdrop of China's domestic politics. I told you last year that the approach of a major leadership transition and China's accession to WTO would soon be coloring all of Beijing's actions. Both of those benchmarks are now upon us. The 16th Communist Party Congress will be held this fall, and China is now confronting the obligations of WTO membership.

On the leadership side, Beijing is likely to be preoccupied this year with succession jockeying, as top leaders decide who will get what positions – and who will retire – at the Party Congress and in the changeover in government positions that will follow next spring. This preoccupation is likely to translate into a cautious and defensive approach on most policy issues. It probably also translates into a persistently nationalist foreign policy, as each of the contenders in the succession contest will be obliged to avoid any hint of being "soft" on the United States.

China's entry into the WTO underscores the trepidation the succession contenders will have about maintaining internal stability. WTO membership is a major challenge to Chinese stability because the economic requirements of accession will upset already disaffected sectors of the population and increase unemployment. If China's leaders stumble in WTO implementation – and even if they succeed – they will face rising socioeconomic tensions at a time when the stakes in the succession contest are pushing them toward a cautious response to problems. In the case of social unrest, that response is more likely to be harsh than accommodative toward the population at large.

The Taiwan issue remains central. Cross-strait relations remain at a stalemate, but there are competing trend lines behind that. Chinese leaders seemed somewhat complacent last year that the growing economic integration across the Taiwan Strait was boosting Beijing's long-term leverage. The results of Taiwan's legislative elections in December, however, strengthened President Chen's hand domestically. Although Beijing's latest policy statement – inviting members of Chen's party to visit the mainland – was designed as a conciliatory gesture, Beijing might resume a more confrontational stance if it suspects him of using his electoral mandate to move toward independence.

Taiwan also remains the focus of China's military modernization programs. Over the past year, Beijing's military training exercises have taken on an increasingly real-world focus, emphasizing rigorous practice in operational capabilities and improving the military's actual ability to use force. This is aimed not only at Taiwan but also at increasing the risk to the United States itself in any future Taiwan contingency. China also continues to upgrade and expand the conventional short-range ballistic missile force it has arrayed against Taiwan.

Beijing also continues to make progress towards fielding its first generation of road mobile strategic missiles – the DF-31. A longer-range version capable of reaching targets in the US will become operational later in the decade.

NORTH KOREA

Staying within East Asia for a moment, let me update you on **North Korea**. The suspension last year of engagement between P'yongyang, Seoul, and Washington reinforced the concerns I cited last year about Kim Chong-il's intentions toward us and our allies in Northeast Asia. Kim's reluctance to pursue constructive dialogue with the South or to undertake meaningful reforms suggests that he remains focused on maintaining internal control – at the expense of addressing the fundamental economic failures that keep the North mired in poverty and pose a long-term threat to the country's stability. North Korea's large standing army continues to be a priority claimant on scarce resources, and we have seen no evidence that P'yongyang has abandoned its goal of eventual reunification of the Peninsula under the North's control.

The cumulative effects of prolonged economic mismanagement have left the country increasingly susceptible to the possibility of state failure. North Korea faces deepening economic deprivation and the return of famine in the absence of fundamental economic reforms and the large-scale international humanitarian assistance it receives – an annual average of 1 million metric tons of food aid over the last five years. It has ignored international efforts to address the systemic agricultural problems that exacerbate the North's chronic food short-ages. Grain production appears to have roughly stabilized, but it still falls far short of the level required to meet minimum nutritional needs for the population. Large numbers of North Koreans face long-term health damage as a result of prolonged malnutrition and collapse of the public health network.

LATIN AMERICA

Other important regions of the developing world are test cases for many of the political, social, and demographic trends I identified earlier – trends that pose latent or growing challenges to US interests, and sometimes fuel terrorists. I have already mentioned Southeast Asia in this respect, citing the rise of Islamic extremism in Indonesia and terrorist links in the Philippines.

Latin America is becoming increasingly volatile as the potential for instability there grows. The region has been whipsawed by five economic crises in as many years, and the economic impact of September 11 worsened an already bleak outlook for regional economies as the global slump reduces demand for exports.

In this context, I am particularly concerned about **Venezuela**, our third largest supplier of petroleum. Domestic unhappiness with President Chavez's "Bolivarian revolution" is growing, economic conditions have deteriorated with the fall in oil prices, and the crisis atmosphere is likely to worsen. In **Argentina**, President Duhalde is trying to maintain public order while putting into place the groundwork for recovery from economic collapse, but his support base is thin.

Colombia too remains highly volatile. The peace process there faces many obstacles, and a significant increase in violence – especially from the FARC – may be in the offing. Colombia's tenuous security situation is taking a toll on the economy and increasing the dangers for US military advisers in the country. Together, the difficult security and economic conditions have hampered Bogota's ability to implement Plan Colombia's counterdrug and social programs. Colombia remains the cornerstone of the world's cocaine trade, and the largest source of heroin for the US market.

AFRICA

The chronic problems of **Sub-Saharan Africa** make it, too, fertile ground for direct and indirect threats to US interests. Governments without accountability and natural disasters have left Africa with the highest concentration of human misery in the world. It is the only region where average incomes have declined since 1970, and Africans have the world's lowest life expectancy at birth. These problems have been compounded by the HIV/AIDS pandemic, which will kill more than 2 million Africans this year, making it the leading source of mortality in the region.

Given these grim facts, the risk of state failures in Sub-Saharan Africa will remain high. In the past decade, the collapse of governments in Somalia, Liberia, Rwanda, Congo-Kinshasa, and elsewhere has led the United States and other international partners to provide hundreds of millions of dollars worth of aid, and to deploy thousands of peacekeepers. A number of other African states – including **Zimbabwe** and **Liberia** – are poised to follow the same downward spiral. In Zimbabwe, President Mugabe's attempts to rig the presidential election scheduled for next month increase the chances of a collapse in law and order that could spill over into South Africa and other neighbors. The UN-monitored truce between Ethiopia and Eritrea also remains fragile.

BALKANS

Finally, let me briefly mention the **Balkans**, the importance of which is underlined by the continuing US military presence there. International peacekeeping troops, with a crucial core from NATO, are key to maintaining stability in the region.

In **Macedonia**, the Framework Agreement brokered by the United States and the EU has eased tensions by increasing the ethnic Albanians' political role, but it remains fragile and most of the agreement has yet to be implemented. Ethnic Slavs are worried about losing their dominance in the country. If they obstruct implementation of the accord, many Albanians could decide that the Slav-dominated government – and by extension the international community – cannot be trusted.

US and other international forces are most at risk in **Bosnia**, where Islamic extremists from outside the region played an important role in the ethnic conflicts of the 1990s. There is considerable sympathy for international Islamic causes among the Muslim community in Bosnia. Some of the mujahedin who fought in the Bosnian wars of the early 1990s stayed there. These factors combine with others present throughout the Balkans – weak border controls, large amounts of weapons, and pervasive corruption and organized crime – to sustain an ongoing threat to US forces there.

CONCLUSION

Mr. Chairman, I want to end my presentation by reaffirming what the President has said on many occasions regarding the threats we face from terrorists and other adversaries. We cannot – and will not – relax our guard against these enemies. If we did so, the terrorists would have won. And that will not happen. The terrorists, rather, should stand warned that we will not falter in our efforts, and in our commitment, until the threat they pose to us has been eliminated.

Thank you, Mr. Chairman. I welcome any questions you and your colleagues have for me.

* * * * * * * *

Adding to the above testimony of the Director of the CIA are the many classified reports that are not made public due to National Security. There is no doubt that terrorist cells are on every continent and operating in every major nation of the world. Some are active but most are silent and laying dormant waiting for the opportunity to strike.

Chapter Seven

Conclusions

And now in closing, the readers must again ask the questions as posed at the beginning of this book:

- Is Islam the kind, loving, caring religion that it claims to be?

- Is Jesus Christ only a prophet and not the Son of God?

- Is Allah the same god as the God of the Bible?

- Is the Koran a friendly, loving, comforting book?

- Are the acts of terrorism around the world justified to promote the casue of Islam?

- Is Islam a political force hiding behind the religion of Allah?

- Is Islam content to live side by side with other religions?

- Can or will Islam be able to willingly co-exist with the other religions of the world?

- Why is America bonded to Israel?

And finally

- Are we closing in on The Last Days as both the Bible and Koran predict?

Bibliography

The Companion Bible King James Version. New Knoxville, OH: American Christian Press.

The Holy Koran (Qur-an), the English translation and authorized by King Fahd Ibu Abdual Aziz Al-Saud, King of the Kingdom of Saudi Arabia. Safa, Raja F. Inside Islam. Charisma House 1996.

Strong, James, S.T.D. LL.D. *Strongs Exhaustive Concordance of the Bible* Peabody, MA: Hendrickson Publishers.

Falwell, James DD, D.Litt., LL.D, Executive Editor *Liberty Annotated Study Bible* 1988.

James Moffatt Translation *The Bible* Grand Rapids, MI: Kregel Publications 1994.

Fox, Everett *The Five Books of Moses* NY: Schocken Books 1995.

Barker, Kenneth, General Editor *New International Version, The NIV Study Bible* Grand Rapids, MI: Zondervan Bible Publishers 1985.

Green, Jay P., General Editor *Interlinear Bible Hebrew-English* Peabody, Massachusetts: Hendrickson Publishers 1989.

Taylor, Ken *The Living Bible* Wheaton, Illinois: Tyndale House Publishers 1973.

The Holy Bible, the original 1611 King James Version authorized by King James of England: Thomas Nelson Publishers 1989.

Worlds Great Religions NY: Time-Life Incorporated 1957.

New American Standard Bible The Lockman Foundation - Foundation Press Publications 1973.

Roberts, J. M. *History of the World* NY: Oxford University Press 1993.

Robinson, B. A., *Ontario Consultants on Religious Tolerance*

Religions of the World

Numbers of adherents; rates of growth

Number of adherents of world religions:

According to David Barrett, et al, editors of the *"World Christian Encyclopedia: A comparative survey of churches and religions - AD 30 to 2200,"* there are 19 major world religions which are subdivided into a total of 270 large religious groups, and many smaller ones. 34,000 separate Christian groups have been identified in the world. *"Over half of them are independent churches that are not interested in linking with the big denominations."* Most people in the world follow one of the religions listed in the following table. Included is the name of the religion, the approximate date of its origin, its main sacred or ethical texts (if any) and its estimated numerical strength (both in absolute numbers and as a percentage of the world's population.)

These data are based on census or public opinion data. [1] **Thus, a person is considered to be of a particular religion if they say that they are of that faith.** Thus, about 88% of the adults in both the U.S. and Canada are Christians. Many individuals and religious groups have much more strict definitions for membership. Many conservative Christians believe that one has to be *"born again"* in order to be counted as a Christian. Using this definition, only about 35% of Americans would be counted as Christians. This difference in definitions between conservative Christians and the rest of the population causes much confusion.

Religion	Date Founded	Sacred Texts	Members	% of World
Chrisitanity	30 CE	The Bible	2,015 million	33% (dropping) 5
Islam	622 CE	Qur'an & Hadith	1,215 million	20% (growing) 5
No religion*	No Date	None	925 million	15% (dropping) 5
Hinduism	1,500 BCE	The Veda	786 million	13% (stable) 5
Buddhism	523 BCE	The Tripitaka	362 million	6% (stable) 5
Atheists	No date	None	211 million	4%
Chinese folk rel.	270 BCE	None	188 million	4%
New Asian rel.	Various	Various	106 million	2%
Tribal Religions	Prehistory	Oral tradition	91 million	2%
Other	Various	Various	19 million	<1%
Sikhism	1500 CE	Guru Granth Sahib	16 million	<1%
Judaism	No consensus	Torah, Talmud	18 million	<1%
Shamanists	Prehistory	Oral Tradition	12 million	<1%
Spiritism			7 million	<1%
Confucianism	520 BCE	Lun Yu	5 million	<1%
Baha'i Faith	1863 CE	Most Holy Book	4 million	<1%
Jainism	570 BCE	Siddhanta, Pakrit	3 million	<1%
Shinto	500 CE	Kojiki, Nohon Shoki	3 million	<1%
Zoroastrianism	No consensus	Avesta	0.2 million	<1%

*Persons with no religion, <u>agnostics</u>, freethinkers, <u>humanists</u>, secularists, etc.

Rate of Change of Christians and Muslims:

Of the two largest religions, the "market share" of Christianity appears to be fairly constant:

■ *U.S. Center for World Mission* estimated in 1997 that the percentage of humans who regard themselves as Christians rose from 33.7% in 1970 to 33.9% in 1996. [2] Its total number of adherents is growing at about 2.3% annually. This is approximately equal to the growth rate of the world's population. Islam is growing faster: about 2.9% and is thus increasing its market share.

■ *"World Christian Encyclopedia: A comparative survey of churches and religions - AD 30 to 2200"*, estimates that as of 2000, Christians make up 33% of the world's population, with close to two billion followers.

■ Author Samuel Huntington disagrees: *"The percentage of Christians in the world peaked at about 30% in the 1980s, leveled off, is now declining, and will probably approximate to about 25% of the world's population by 2025. As a result of their extremely high rates of population growth, the proportion of Muslims in the world will continue to increase dramatically, amounting to 20 percent of the world's population about the turn of the century, surpassing the number of Christians some years later, and probably accounting for about 30 percent of the world's population by 2025."* [3]

■ The *UK Christian Handbook* has lower figures. They estimate that 28.3% of the world's population identified themselves as Christians in 1990. They expect this to drop to 27.7% by the year 2000, and to 27.1 in 2010. [4] They attribute the drop to the lower birth rate among Christians compared to followers of other religions.

Within Christianity, not all denominations have the same growth rate. Some annual growth rates are:

■ Pentecostals: 8.1%
■ Evangelicals: 5.4%
■ All Protestants: 3.3%
■ Roman Catholics and Others: 1.3%

Since the growth rate of humanity is above 1.4%, the "market share" of Roman Catholicism appears to be dropping.

Missiologist Ralph Winter estimated in early 2001 that there are 680 million *"born again"* Christians in the world, and that they are growing at about 7% a year. This represents about 11% of the world's population and 33% of the total number of Christians. [6]

Reference books on world religion:

The ultimate reference book is the two volume monumental set, World Christian Encyclopedia, released in mid-2001, by Oxford University Press. It contains 1699 pages with information about religion in the 238 countries of the world:

- David Barrett et al, *"World Christian Encyclopedia: A comparative survey of churches and religions - AD 30 to 2200,"* Oxford University Press, (2001). Read reviews or order this book safely from Amazon.com online book store.

References used in the above essay:

1. J. W. Wright, Editor, *"The Universal Almanac, 1996",* Andrews & McMeel, Kansas City.
2. Greg H. Parsons, Executive Director, *"U. S. Center for World Mission,"* Pasadena, CA; quoted in Zondervan News Service, 1997-FEB-21.
3. Samuel Huntington, *"The Clash of Civilizations and the remaking of world order,"* Touchstone Books, (1998), pages 65 to 66. Read reviews or order this book safely from Amazon.com online book store. This is a controversial book which argues that world divisions in the future will be based on culture, ethnicity and religion.
4. Quoted in *Religion Today's* Current News Summary for 1999-OCT-19.
5. Based on 2000-JAN data from the *Global Evangelization Movement* as reported in *Religion Today* on 2000-JAN-10. They are based on a total world's population of 6,091,351,000 people.
6. *"Jesus Christ known to 11% of world's population,"* Religion Today, 2001-JAN-25, at: http://news.crosswalk.com/religion/item/

This Report Includes All The Countries of the World and Shows How Many Muslims Are In Each One

Country Name	Total Population	Muslims Percentage	Number of Muslims
Afghanistan	22,664,136	100%	22,664,136
Albania	3,249,136	75%	2,436,852
Algeria	29,183,032	99%	28,891,202
Angola	10,342,899	25%	2,585,725
Antiqua & Barbuda	65,647	n/a	
Argentina	34,672,997	2	693,460
Aruba	67,794	5	3,390
Australia	18,260,863	2.09	382,000
Azerbaijan	7,676,953	93.4	7,170,274
Bahrain	590,042	100	590,042
Benin	5,709,529	15	856,429
Bangladesh	123,062,800	85	104,603,380
Bhutan	1,822,625	5	91,131
Bosnia & Herzegovina	2,656,240	40	1,062,496
Botswana	1,477,630	5	73,882
Brazil	162,661,214	0.6	1,000,000
Brunei	299,939	63	188,962
Bulgaria	8,612,757	14	1,205,786
Burkina Faso	10,623,323	50	5,311,662
Burma	45,975,625	10	4,597,563
Burundi	5,943,057	20	1,188,611
Cambodia	10,861,218	1	108,612
Cameroon	14,261,557	55	7,843,856
Canada	28,820,671	1.48	400,000

Country Name	Total Population	Muslims Percentage	Number of Muslims
Central African Rep.	3,274,426	55	1,800,934
Chad	6,976,845	85	5,930,318
China	1,210,004,956	11	133,100,545
Christmas Island	813	10	81
Cocos (Keeling) Island	609	57	347
Comoros	569,237	86	489,544
Congo	2,527,841	15	379,176
Cote d'Ivoire	14,762,445	60	8,857,467
Croatia	5,004,112	1.2	60,049
Cyprus	744,609	33	245,721
Djibouti	427,642	94	401,983
Egypt	63,575,107	94	59,760,601
Equatorial Guinea	431,282	25	107,821
Eritrea	3,427,883	80	2,742,306
Ethiopia	57,171,662	65	37,161,580
Fiji	782,381	11	86,062
France	58,317,450	7	4,082,222
Gabon	1,172,798	1	11,728
Gambia	1,204,984	90	1,084,486
Gaza Strip	923,940	98.7	911,929
Georgia	5,219,810	11	574,179
Germany	83,536,115	3.4	2,840,228
Ghana	17,698,271	30	5,309,481
Gibraltar	28,765	8	2,301
Greece	10,538,594	1.5	158,079
Guinea	7,411,981	95	7,041,382
Guinea-Bissau	1,151,330	70	805,931
Guyana	712,091	15	106,814
Hong Kong	6,305,413	1	63,054
India	952,107,694	14	133,295,077

Country Name	Total Population	Muslims Percentage	Number of Muslims
Indonesia	206,611,600	95	196,281,020
Iran	66,094,264	99	65,433,321
Iraq	21,422,292	97	20,779,623
Israel	5,421,995	14	759,079
Italy	57,460,274	1	574,603
Japan	125,449,703	1	1,254,497
Jordan	4,212,152	95	4,001,544
Kazakstan	16,916,463	51.2	8,661,229
Kenya	28,176,686	29.5	8,312,122
Kuwait	1,950,047	89	1,735,542
Kyrgyzstan	4,529,648	76.1	3,447,062
Lebanon	3,776,317	70	2,643,422
Liberia	2,109,789	30	632,937
Libya	5,445,436	100	5,445,436
Lesotho	1,970,781	10	197,078
Macedonia	2,104,035	30	631,211
Madagascar	13,670,507	20	2,734,101
Malaysia	19,962,893	52	10,380,704
Maldives	270,758	100	270,758
Mali	9,653,261	90	8,687,935
Malta	375,576	14	52,581
Mauritania	2,336,048	100	2,336,048
Mauritius	1,140,256	19.5	222,350
Mayotte	100,838	99	99,830
Mongolia	2,496,617	4	99,865
Morocco	29,779,156	98.7	29,392,027
Mozambique	17,877,927	29	5,184,599
Namibia	1,677,243	5	83,862
Nepal	22,094,033	4	883,761
Netherlands	15,568,034	3	467,041

Country Name	Total Population	Muslims Percentage	Number of Muslims
Niger	9,113,001	91	8,292,831
Nigeria	103,912,489	75	77,934,367
Norway	4,438,547	1.5	66,578
Oman	2,186,548	100	2,186,548
Pakistan	129,275,660	97	125,397,390
Panama	2,655,094	4	106,204
Philippines	74,480,848	14	10,427,319
Qatar	547,761	100	547,761
Reunion	679,198	20	135,840
Romania	21,657,162	20	4,331,432
Russia	148,178,487	18	26,672,127
Rwanda	6,853,359	1	68,534
Saudi Arabia	19,409,058	100	19,409,058
Senegal	9,092,749	95	8,638,112
Serbia & Montenegro	10,614,558	19	2,016,766
Sierra Leone	4,793,121	65	3,115,529
Singapore	3,396,924	17	577,477
Slovenia	1,951,443	1	19,514
Somalia	9,639,151	100	9,639,151
South Africa	41,743,459	2	834,869
Sri Lanka	18,553,074	9	1,669,777
Sudan	31,547,543	85	26,815,412
Suriname	436,418	25	109,105
Swaziland	998,730	10	99,873
Sweden	9,800,000	3.6	320,000
Tajikistan	5,916,373	85	5,028,917
Tanzania	29,058,470	65	18,888,006
Thailand	58,851,357	14	8,239,190
Togo	4,570,530	55	2,513,792
Trinidad & Tobago	1,272,385	12	152,686

Country Name	Total Population	Muslims Percentage	Number of Muslims
Tunisia	9,019,687	98	8,839,293
Turkey	62,484,478	99.8	62,359,509
Turkmenistan	4,149,283	87	3,609,876
Uganda	20,158,176	36	7,256,943
United Arab Emirates	3,057,337	96	2,935,044
United Kingdom	58,489,975	2.7	1,579,229
United States	266,476,278	3.75	9,992,860
Uzbekistan	23,418,381	88	20,608,175
West Bank	1,427,741	75	1,070,806
Western Sahara	222,631	100	222,631
Yemen	13,483,178	99	13,348,346
Zaire	46,498,539	10	4,649,854
Zambia	9,159,072	15	1,373,861
Zimbabwe	11,271,314	15	1,690,697

CIA: The World Factbook 2001
www.cia.gov/cia/publications

MUSLIM POPULATION
Approx. 1.3 Billion

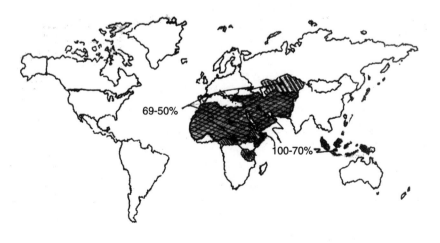

Muslims Population

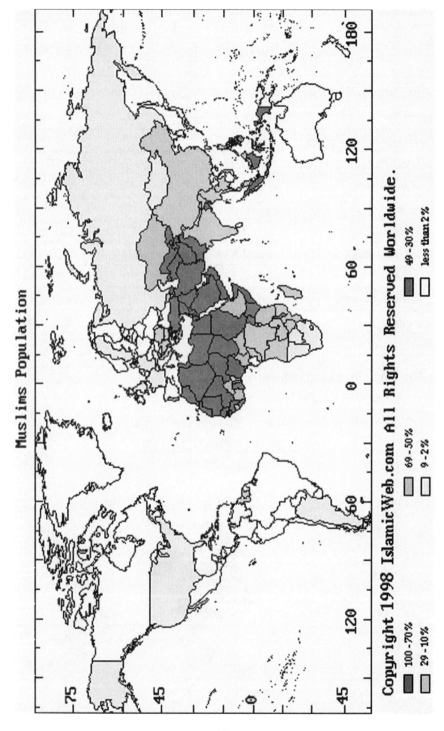

100 - 70%   69 - 50%   49 - 30%
29 - 10%   9 - 2%   less than 2%

152

– NOTES –

– NOTES –

– NOTES –

– NOTES –